University of Kentucky Wildcats Basketball IQ:

The Ultimate Test of True Fandom

JOEL KATTE

Cataloging-in-Publication Data is available from the Library of Congress.
ISBN: 978-0-9912699-3-8
First edition, first printing.

Cover artwork courtesy of Jason Prigge.
www.priggeart.com

Back cover photos courtesy Alyson Bridgewater Drumm and Angela Ingram
Gallagher.

Cover design by Holly Walden Ross.
Interior design and layout by BMP Digital.

Black Mesa Publishing, LLC
Florida

admin@blackmesabooks.com
www.blackmesabooks.com

BLACK MESA IQ TITLES

Mixed Martial Arts (Vol. 1 & 2)
Atlanta Braves
New York Yankees
Georgia Bulldogs Football
Boston Celtics (Vol. 1 & 2)
Florida Gators Football
Milwaukee Brewers
St. Louis Cardinals (Vol. 1 & 2)
Major League Baseball
Boston Red Sox (Vol. 1 & 2)
Tampa Bay Rays
Oklahoma Sooners Football
Texas Longhorns Football
Texas A&M Aggies Football
Cincinnati Reds
New England Patriots
West Point Football
Rock & Roll Music
Buffalo Bills
Kentucky Derby
NHL Hockey
The Beatles
Cleveland Indians
Miami Hurricanes Football
Baltimore Orioles
Green Bay Packers
Los Angeles Dodgers
Kansas City Royals
Pittsburgh Pirates
San Francisco Giants

This book is dedicated to the crazy, passionate University of Kentucky Wildcats basketball fans! We all are truly the ultimate of the ultimate sports fans. Big Blue Nation is worldwide but occupies most of its space in fans' hearts, bleeding blue 24 hours a day, 7 days a week, 365 days a year!

I hope this book will fuel your passion because it is this passion that will continue to attract the best players, electrify Rupp Arena like no other place, and lift the program to more national championships.

CONTENTS

	INTRODUCTION	1
1	LIVING THE DREAM	5
2	THE CHAMPIONSHIPS	9
3	THROUGH THE YEARS	21
4	THE LEGENDS	35
5	THE CALIPARI ERA	61
6	THE RECORDS	97
7	THE COACHES	107
8	50-50 BALLS	125
	BONUS: KENTUCKY DERBY IQ	133
	JOEL KATTE	149
	BLACK MESA	151

University of Kentucky Wildcats Basketball

"The one thing people have always enjoyed emotionally is Kentucky basketball. Cal has brought that (joy) back and given people some pride in their program again. He's given them energy and fun and I don't know how you put a price tag on that."
— Mitch Barnhart, U.K. Athletic Director

INTRODUCTION

The most beloved college basketball team of all-time is the University of Kentucky Wildcats. No Division 1 college program has won more basketball games than U.K. Big Blue Nation extends far beyond Lexington, Kentucky. Loyal fans across the nation bleed blue and cheer their team on intensely year after year. Because the state of Kentucky does not have any professional sports teams, a Wildcats fan's commitment to the team is year-round. Fans go online to follow the team's potential recruits, watching YouTube highlight clips and reading high school box scores from teams around the world. Fans wait anxiously to hear about recruits' commitments to Kentucky. When players commit to U.K., their names are added to a very special group of players known as "Next Cats".

The "Next Cats" are often high school All-Americans who are only a year or two away from being NBA draft picks. Fans camp outside Rupp Arena to buy tickets for an always sold-out Big Blue Madness event that is held every October for fans to catch their first glimpse of the Wildcats in action at Rupp Arena.

All year-round Kentuckians wear U.K. blue. On game days, schools, offices and grocery stores are a sea of blue. Some have described U.K. fandom as a religion, and recently someone declared, "Saying anything bad about Kentucky basketball to a fan is like swearing in church."

Think you know Wildcats history?

Think again.

The 505 Questions in *University of Kentucky Wildcats Basketball IQ: The Ultimate Test of True Fandom* will test the most hardcore Kentucky fans. Regardless of your performance, go back and reread each chapter and memorize every fun, fascinating Wildcats fact to impress your friends and families at your next March Madness party or tailgate outing. If you are fortunate enough to attend a game at Rupp Arena after reading this book, your blue and white face-painted head will be filled with important U.K. basketball memories to share with the fans of all ages sitting around you. When you can correctly answer 90% or more of the book's 505 questions, you have achieved ultimate fan status!

"We feel that every boy who puts on a Kentucky uniform just plays a little better than he would in one of another color."
— Adolph Rupp

1 LIVING THE DREAM

Every kid who falls in love with basketball dreams of playing in the NBA. Many kids grow up picturing themselves cutting the lane in New York's Madison Square Garden or throwing one down in Chicago's United Center like the legend Michael Jordan or like one of today's superstars LeBron James, Kevin Durant or Anthony Davis.

Playing park basketball is magical too. Not every kid will experience the thrill of crashing the courts at Venice Beach in Los Angeles or Rucker Park in Harlem, but each of us can walk over to our local park bouncing a ball, pulling others in for a quick pick-up challenge.

Making backyard ball memories with family and neighbors is some of the most special time shared with those we love. Carefree timelessness of playing, sweating, and imagining you're wearing Boston Celtic green in The Garden while Dad blocks your shot as if he is the great Wilt "The Stilt" Chamberlain or Kareem Abdul-Jabbar is priceless! You will likely hold these memories closely for the rest of your life.

However, the dream is most real and can only be realized when it's just the baller and the hoop. The daily discipline of practice, visioning, and outworking the rest of the best is the only route to Rupp Arena and the only winning combination to become a lottery pick in the NBA draft.

Let's start by honoring the Wildcats who have lived this dream!

QUESTIONS 1-15

Q1: Name the Wildcats who were selected in the NBA draft as the number one pick.

Q2: What Wildcats were selected in the NBA draft as number two picks?

Q3: What NBA team made Rick Robey the third pick in the 1978 draft?
  a) Atlanta Hawks
  b) Indiana Pacers
  c) Buffalo Braves
  d) Seattle Supersonics

Q4: Name the Wildcat who was selected fourth in the 1993 NBA draft.

Q5: What two Wildcats were selected fifth in the NBA draft?

Q6: How many Wildcats have been selected sixth in the NBA draft?

Q7: Name the Wildcat who was inducted into the Naismith Memorial Basketball Hall of Fame in 2008 and was selected seventh by the San Diego Rockets in the 1967 draft.

Q8: What Wildcats fan favorites were selected eighth in the NBA draft?

Q9: Name all five of the 2010 Wildcats who were selected as first round draft picks.

Q10: How many Wildcats were selected in the first and second rounds of the 2012 NBA draft? You earn all-star status with this question if you can name the players and the teams that selected them.

Q11: Anthony Davis and Michael Kidd-Gilchrist were selected number one and two in the 2012 NBA draft. Has this ever happened before or since?

Q12: True or False: Sam Bowie was the second pick in the 1984 NBA draft. Michael Jordan was the number one pick that year.

Q13: What team selected Julius Randle seventh in the 2014 NBA draft?

Q14: How many Wildcats were drafted in 1949, 1960, 1975, 1978 and 1996?

Q15: What was unique about Johnny Cox being drafted by the New York Knicks in 1958 and Roger Newman being selected by the Boston Celtics in 1960?

ANSWERS 1-15

A1: John Wall (Washington Wizards, 2010), Anthony Davis (New Orleans Hornets, 2012), Karl-Anthony Towns (Minnesota Timberwolves, 2015).

A2: Sam Bowie (Portland Trailblazers, 1984), Michael Kidd-Gilchrist (Charlotte Bobcats, 2012), Tom Payne (Atlanta Hawks, 1971 NBA Supplemental Hardship Draft).

A3: B. Indiana Pacers.

A4: Jamal Mashburn.

A5: Kenny Walker (New York Knicks, 1986), DeMarcus Cousins (Sacramento Kings, 2010).

A6: Five. Melvin Turpin (Washington Bullets, 1984), Antoine Walker (Boston Celtics, 1996), Ron Mercer (Boston Celtics, 1997), Nerlens Noel (New Orleans Pelicans, 2013), Willie Cauley-Stein (Sacramento Kings, 2015).

A7: Pat Riley.

A8: Rex Chapman (Charlotte Hornets, 1988), Brandon Knight (Detroit Pistons, 2011).

A9: John Wall (Washington Wizards), DeMarcus Cousins (Sacramento Kings), Patrick Patterson (Houston Rockets), Eric Bledsoe (Oklahoma City Thunder), Daniel Orton (Orlando Magic).

A10: Six. Anthony Davis (New Orleans Hornets), Michael Kidd-Gilchrist (Charlotte Bobcats), Terrence Jones (Houston Rockets), Marquis Teague (Chicago Bulls), Doron Lamb (Milwaukee Bucks), Darius Miller (New Orleans Hornets).

A11: No.

A12: False. Michael Jordan was the third overall draft pick. Sam Bowie was picked second. Hakeem Olajuwon was selected first by the Houston Rockets.

A13: Julius Randle was picked seventh by the Los Angeles Lakers.

A14: Four.

A15: They were the first juniors eligible for the draft.

"I can predict with certainty whatever region we're in will be the toughest region because it is every year. Who has the best shot at beating Kentucky? They'll all be lining up. I'm worried they're going to try to stick an NBA team in there."
— John Calipari

2 THE CHAMPIONSHIPS

Kentucky is the only school to win multiple NCAA and NIT championships. Only UCLA has won more NCAA national titles than U.K. No school has more NCAA Tournament appearances and wins than Kentucky, and no team has had more Sweet Sixteen and Elite Eight appearances than the Wildcats.

Simply put, the Wildcats have won more trophies, cut down more nets, and painted and displayed more historic game balls than any other college program in the nation!

QUESTIONS 16-30

Q16: How many NCAA national titles has U.K. won?

Q17: Name the first U.K. NCAA championship team.
  a) 1945-46
  b) 1946-47
  c) 1947-48
  d) 1948-49

Q18: True or False: U.K.'s first two championships were back-to-back titles.

Q19: True or False: When the Wildcats won their first NCAA championship, they became the first team to win both the NIT and the NCAA.

Q20: Who was the high scorer in U.K.'s first national championship win over Baylor?
  a) Wallace "Wah Wah" Jones
  b) Alex Groza
  c) Ralph Beard
  d) Kenneth Rollins

Q21: What was the final record of U.K.'s first championship team?
  a) 35-1
  b) 34-2
  c) 33-3
  d) 32-4

Q22: The Wildcats beat the Oklahoma A&M Aggies 46-36 in Seattle to win their second NCAA championship. How many field goals did the Wildcats hold the Aggies to in the title game?
  a) 12
  b) 11
  c) 10
  d) 9

Q23: Alex Groza was the Wildcats high scorer in their second championship title game. How many of the Wildcats 46 points did Groza score?
  a) 25
  b) 22
  c) 19

d) 16

Q24: True or False: U.K.'s second championship team led the Oklahoma A&M Aggies the entire game.

Q25: How many healthy players helped the 1950-51 Wildcats win their third NCAA championship?
a) 5
b) 6
c) 7
d) 8

Q26: Name the team U.K. defeated 68-58 to win its third championship.
a) Seattle
b) Kansas
c) Kansas State
d) Wisconsin

Q27: What Wildcat scored nine points with an infected throat, proving to be instrumental in U.K.'s third championship game?
a) Walt Hirsch
b) Bill Spivey
c) Cliff Hagan
d) Shelby Linville

Q28: U.K. won its fourth national title on March 22, 1958, beating Seattle 84-72. Where was this game played?

Q29: Name the Seattle player who scored 25 points and grabbed 19 rebounds vs. U.K. in that same title game.

Q30: Name the Wildcat who scored a game-high 30 points against Seattle.
a) Vernon Hatton
b) Johnny Cox
c) John Crigler
d) Don Mills

ANSWERS 16-30

A16: Eight.

A17: C. U.K.'s first national championship was 1947-48.

A18: True. U.K.'s first two championships were back-to-back.

A19: False. They became the second team to win the NIT and NCAA championships. U.K. won the NIT in 1946.

A20: B. Alex Groza was the high scorer with 14 points.

A21: B. 34-2.

A22: D. Nine.

A23: A. 25.

A24: False. The Aggies led 5-2, but then the Wildcats scored seven straight points and led the rest of the game.

A25: B. Six.

A26: C. Kansas State.

A27: C. Cliff Hagan.

A28: Louisville.

A29: Elgin Baylor.

A30: A. Vernon Hatton.

QUESTIONS 31-45

Q31: What was the largest deficit U.K. faced in its 1958 title game vs. Seattle?
a) 6
b) 7
c) 9
d) 11

Q32: U.K. trailed Seattle most of the game. When did the Wildcats take their first lead with a Don Mills hook shot?
a) 5:36 left in the first half
b) 15:07 left in the game
c) 10:57 left in the game
d) 6:08 left in the game

Q33: John Crigler contributed 14 points in the Wildcat's fourth championship win. How many rebounds did he grab?
a) 10
b) 12
c) 14
d) 16

Q34: What team did U.K. beat on March 27, 1978, in St. Louis to win its fifth NCAA championship?
a) North Carolina
b) Duke
c) Indiana
d) UCLA

Q35: Name the senior Wildcat whose legendary 41 point performance prompted 18,271 fans in St. Louis to chant, "Goose, Goose."
a) Rick Robey
b) Jack Givens
c) Kyle Macy
d) Truman Claytor

Q36: On April 1, 1996, the Wildcats defeated the Syracuse Orangeman 76-67 for their sixth NCAA championship. Where was the game played?

Q37: Tony Delk, the Final Four's Most Outstanding Player, led the Wildcats with 24 points. How many of his 24 points were three-pointers?
a) 5
b) 6

c) 7

d) 8

Q38: What 1996 freshman joined Delk on the Final Four All-Tournament team after scoring a career-high 20 points coming off the bench?

a) Anthony Epps

b) Antoine Walker

c) Ron Mercer

d) Mark Pope

Q39: The next few questions are about the 1997-98 Kentucky team that overcame a halftime deficit to Utah and won the seventh NCAA championship in school history. How many points were the Wildcats down to the Utes at halftime?

a) 10

b) 11

c) 12

d) 13

Q40: How many fans watched the Wildcats win their seventh national championship in San Antonio's Alamodome?

a) 28,788

b) 33,653

c) 40,509

d) 51,255

Q41: By what margin did the Utes out rebound the Wildcats in the first half?

a) 21-7

b) 24-6

c) 19-9

d) 17-8

Q42: Who helped inspire the "Comeback Cats" by scoring seven straight points early in the second half?

a) Wayne Turner

b) Nazr Mohammed

c) Jamaal Magloire

d) Heshimu Evans

Q43: What Wildcat hit a baseline jump shot to give the Wildcats a 65-64 lead over the Utes with 4:54 left in the game?

a) Scott Padgett

b) Jeff Sheppard

c) Cameron Mills

d) Wayne Turner

Q44: Name the Wildcat who earned the Final Four Most Outstanding Player award, and the other Wildcat who joined him on the All-Final Four team after scoring 17 points in the 1998 title game.

Q45: Coming down the stretch, the tired Utes missed an astounding number of consecutive field goals. How many shots did they miss in a row?
   a) 9
   b) 10
   c) 11
   d) 12

ANSWERS 31-45

A31: D. 11. U.K. trailed Seattle by 11 twice and battled back both times.

A32: D. With 6:08 left in the game, a Don Mills hook shot put U.K. up 61-60. The Wildcats led the rest of the game.

A33: C. 14. Crigler grabbed 14 rebounds to go with his 14 points.

A34: B. Duke.

A35: B. Jack Givens.

A36: Meadowlands in East Rutherford, New Jersey.

A37: C. Tony Delk drained an NCAA championship game record-tying seven three-pointers.

A38: C. Ron Mercer.

A39: A. Ten. U.K. was the first team in NCAA championship game history to overcome a double-digit halftime deficit. The Wildcats trailed 41-31.

A40: C. 40,509 fans.

A41: B. 24-6.

A42: D. Heshimu Evans.

A43: B. Jeff Sheppard.

A44: Jeff Sheppard was the Outstanding Player of the Tournament and Scott Padgett was named to the All-Final Four Team.

A45: C. The Utes missed 11 consecutive shots.

QUESTIONS 46-55

Q46: The next few questions are about the 2011-12 NCAA champion Wildcats. What was U.K.'s overall won-loss record that season?
a) 38-2
b) 37-3
c) 36-4
d) 35-5

Q47: How many points did the Most Outstanding Player Anthony Davis score in that season's title game?
a) 6
b) 9
c) 12
d) 14

Q48: How many rebounds did Davis grab?
a) 10
b) 12
c) 13
d) 16

Q49: How many shots did Davis block?
a) 4
b) 5
c) 6
d) 7

Q50: How many times did a Wildcat block a Jayhawks shot?
a) 10
b) 11
c) 12
d) 13

Q51: Name the Wildcat who was the highest scorer in the title game.
a) Michael Kidd-Gilchrist
b) Doron Lamb
c) Marquis Teague
d) Terrence Jones

Q52: Anthony Davis and Terrence Jones held Kansas Jayhawks lottery pick and AP All-American Thomas Robinson to 6 of 17 shooting for 18 points. How many rebounds did Robinson secure?
a) 10

b) 12
c) 15
d) 17

Q53: Coach John Calipari avenged a title game loss to Kansas and coach Bill Self. What year did Calipari's Memphis Tigers come up just short of a NCAA championship?
a) 2006
b) 2007
c) 2008
d) 2009

Q54: Name the teams that beat the 2011-12 NCAA champions.

Q55: Where was the 2012 NCAA championship game held?

ANSWERS 46-55

A46: A. 38-2.

A47: A. Six. Anthony Davis was only 1 for 10 from the field.

A48: D. 16 rebounds.

A49: C. Six. Davis also added five assists and three steals.

A50: B. 11 blocks.

A51: B. Lamb scored 22 of Kentucky's 67 points.

A52: D. 17 rebounds.

A53: C. 2008.

A54: Indiana and Vanderbilt.

A55: Superdome in New Orleans, Louisiana.

"We are the gold standard—not just for college basketball, but for all of college athletics."
— John Calipari

3 THROUGH THE YEARS

It is not possible to capture every magical moment and historical statistic in over 113 years of Kentucky basketball; however, a glimpse through the years allows the reader to see the evolution of the game, the building of an elite program, and the crafting of a fun-filled fan experience. The Kentucky players and fans of 1903, not too far removed from basketball inventor James Naismith's peach baskets, could not have imagined fireworks being shot up into Rupp Arena nor could they have thought it would be possible to play exhibition games in the Bahamas. Today's fans can only dream up a bigger stage and experience for the next decades' "Next Cats".

QUESTIONS 56-70

Q56: State College (Kentucky) recorded its first franchise win on February 18, 1903, over the Lexington YMCA. What was the Wildcats record that first season?

Q57: In 1909, the Wildcats finished the season with their first winning record. What was their final record?

Q58: On March 1, 1912, Kentucky finished the season with a perfect 9-0 record. Name the team they beat to complete their perfect season.

Q59: In 1921, Kentucky defeated Tulane, Mercer, Mississippi A&M and Georgia to win the first Southern Intercollegiate Athletic Association basketball championship, which is believed to be the first ever college basketball tournament. How did Kentucky fans hear about and celebrate this first championship?

Q60: Name the Wildcat who became Kentucky's first All-American basketball player in 1921.

Q61: What team did U.K. defeat on January 21, 1922, to record the 100th victory in school history?

Q62: On December 13, 1924, the Wildcats beat Cincinnati. What was significant about that game?

Q63: On March 21, 1930, Kentucky named high school coach Adolph Rupp its next head coach. Where was the high school that Coach Rupp was moving from?
   a) Green Bay, Wisconsin
   b) Freeport, Illinois
   c) Milwaukee, Wisconsin
   d) St. Louis, Missouri

Q64: Name the team U.K. defeated to record Coach Rupp's first win on December 18, 1930.

Q65: On February 28, 1933, U.K. beat Mississippi State 46-27 to win its first Southeastern Conference Tournament championship. Where was the game played?

Q66: On February 17, 1934, Wildcat fans nearly rioted as they jockeyed for seats at the Alumni Gymnasium. What was so significant about this game?

Q67: On February 14, 1938, Joe Hagan hit a 48-foot shot with only 12 seconds left in the game to help U.K. beat Marquette 35-33. How did Governor A.B. "Happy" Chandler honor this historic shot after the game?

Q68: U.K. won its first ever NCAA championship game in 1942. Prior to their big win they also won an SEC championship. How many SEC championships did that give the Wildcats at that point?

a) 4
b) 5
c) 6
d) 7

Q69: What team stopped U.K. from winning back-to-back NIT championships on March 24, 1947, in Madison Square Garden in front of a record crowd of 18,493 fans?

a) Rhode Island
b) Utah
c) Cincinnati
d) Louisville

Q70: How many fans honored Adolph Rupp's "Fabulous Five" 1948 NCAA champions with a Lexington fire truck parade?

a) 12,000
b) 15,000
c) 18,000
d) 19,000

ANSWERS 56-70

A56: The Wildcats first season record in 1903 was 1-2.

A57: The Wildcats first winning record was 5-4 in 1909.

A58: Kentucky beat Georgetown College 19-18 to complete a perfect 9-0 1912 season.

A59: Hundreds of fans received play-by-play messages via telegraph. Fans greeted the team when the train arrived in Lexington. The celebration continued with a downtown parade.

A60: Basil Hayden.

A61: Louisville.

A62: The Wildcats' win over Cincinnati was the first game played in the school's new 2,800 seat $100,000 Alumni Gymnasium.

A63: B. Freeport, Illinois.

A64: Georgetown College.

A65: Atlanta, Georgia.

A66: U.K. recorded its national record 23rd consecutive win with its 47-27 win over Vanderbilt.

A67: Governor A. B. "Happy" Chandler celebrated Joe Hagan's 48-foot game-winning basket by pounding a nail into the floor to mark the spot of the incredible shot.

A68: C. Six.

A69: B. Utah. Wat Misaka's defense kept Ralph Beard to only two points as Utah defeated Kentucky.

A70: B. 15,000.

QUESTIONS 71-85

Q71: "The Fabulous Five" played on the 1948 U.S. Olympic gold medal-winning basketball team. Where were the 1948 Summer Olympics held?
a) London
b) Helsinki
c) Melbourne
d) Rome

Q72: The AP released its first Top 25 basketball poll on January 20, 1949. True or False: U.K. finished the 1949 season ranked number one in the AP Top 25.

Q73: On December 1, 1950, U.K. played its first game in the 11,500 seat Memorial Coliseum. Some people called the new facility a "White Elephant." How much did Memorial Coliseum cost?
a) $1.7 million
b) $2.1 million
c) $3.3 million
d) $3.9 million

Q74: Cawood Ledford is one of U.K.'s greatest basketball legends because of the four thrilling decades he spent as the Wildcats' radio play-by-play announcer. What year did Ledford call his first U.K. basketball game?

Q75: Kentucky defeated LSU 63-56 in a 1954 SEC playoff game to complete a perfect season. What was their record?
a) 24-0
b) 25-0
c) 26-0
d) 27-0

Q76: Georgia Tech shocked U.K. fans with a 59-58 upset over the beloved Wildcats in Memorial Coliseum on January 8, 1955. What made this loss extra devastating?

Q77: On December 7, 1957, the Wildcats defeated Temple 85-83 in three overtimes. Who scored the last six points for the Wildcats in what became known as the "longest game in U.K. history"?
a) Vernon Hatton
b) John Crigler
c) Johnny Cox
d) Adrian Smith

Q78: The 1958 NCAA champions—known as "The Fiddlin' Five"—gave U.K. its fourth national title. What made this win so significant for Coach Rupp?

Q79: Who beat the number one ranked "Rupp's Runts" in the 1966 NCAA national title game in what is considered one of the greatest upsets in Tournament history?

Q80: On January 27, 1968, U.K. beat a team 121-95. Name the team they beat and the opposing player who scored a record-setting 52 points.

Q81: What team did U.K. beat on January 18, 1969, to become the first team in college basketball history to win 1,000 games?
    a) Auburn
    b) Tennessee
    c) Florida
    d) Missouri

Q82: Who is the All-American from Louisville that committed to Kentucky on June 9, 1969, becoming the first black player to sign with the Wildcats?

Q83: Who became the first Wildcat to score 2,000 points?

Q84: What team upset the Wildcats 106-100 in a 1970 NCAA Tournament game?
    a) Texas
    b) Jacksonville
    c) Kansas
    d) UCLA

Q85: Adolph Rupp's last game was a 1972 NCAA Tournament 73-54 loss to what team?
    a) Wisconsin
    b) UCLA
    c) Florida State
    d) Indiana

ANSWERS 71-85

A71: A. London. The United States beat France 64-21 at Wembley Stadium.

A72: True.

A73: D. $3.9 million.

A74: 1953.

A75: B. 25-0.

A76: Georgia Tech's win snapped U.K.'s remarkable national record 129-game home winning streak.

A77: A. Vernon Hatton. On March 21, 1958, Hatton scored with 17 seconds left to lift Kentucky over Temple 61-60, catapulting the Wildcats into the NCAA championship game.

A78: The 1958 NCAA championship win was particularly special to Coach Rupp since he vowed to win another title after Kentucky's 1953 season was suspended.

A79: Texas Western upset Kentucky 72-65.

A80: LSU. "Pistol" Pete Maravich scored 52 points against the Wildcats.

A81: B. Tennessee.

A82: Tom Payne.

A83: Dan Issel.

A84: B. Jacksonville.

A85: C. Florida State.

QUESTIONS 86-100

Q86: Coach Joe B. Hall and his Wildcats won the SEC championship in his first season. What was their 1972-73 record?
a) 18-12
b) 22-8
c) 24-6
d) 25-5

Q87: On March 22, 1975, the Wildcats beat undefeated Indiana to advance to the Final Four. To what team did U.K. lose 92-85 in the title game?
a) UTEP
b) UCLA
c) North Carolina
d) Duke

Q88: Jack Givens led a late rally that propelled the Wildcats to a 94-93 overtime win in the last regular season game played at Memorial Coliseum on March 8, 1976. Who was U.K.'s opponent?
a) LSU
b) Mississippi State
c) Vanderbilt
d) Georgia Tech

Q89: The first game played at Rupp Arena was on November 27, 1976. The Wildcats won 72-64. Who did they beat?
a) Wisconsin
b) Minnesota
c) Michigan State
d) Northwestern

Q90: How many seats were in Rupp Arena when it opened?
a) 19,000
b) 21,000
c) 23,000
d) 24,000

Q91: How much did it cost to build Rupp Arena?
a) $40 million
b) $45 million
c) $50 million
d) $55 million

Q92: Who scored the first basket in Rupp Arena?

Q93: What was so significant about top-ranked Kentucky's game against Kansas on December 10, 1977?

Q94: On March 27, 1978, Jack Givens scored 41 points vs. Duke as the Wildcats won their fifth national championship. What was Givens' nickname?

Q95: On March 26, 1983, U.K. beat Louisville to advance to the Final Four. How many years had it been since these two Kentucky teams played each other?
   a) 15
   b) 19
   c) 22
   d) 24

Q96: Georgetown University beat the Wildcats in the 1984 semifinal game. U.K. was hurt by an impressive second half run by the Hoyas. How many of the first 25 points scored in the second half did Georgetown score?
   a) 19
   b) 21
   c) 23
   d) 25

Q97: On March 2, 1991, Kentucky beat Auburn 114-93 at Rupp Arena in front of 24,310 fans. What was significant about this game?

Q98: What team knocked Jamal Mashburn and the Wildcats out of the 1993 Final Four? HINT: They were known as "The Fab Five".

Q99: On February 15, 1997, the Wildcats beat LSU 99-95 to complete the greatest comeback in U.K. history. By how many points did the Wildcats trail with 15:34 left in the game?
   a) 27
   b) 29
   c) 31
   d) 33

Q100: The Wildcats beat Vanderbilt 101-63 on March 2, 1996, to finish the season with a perfect 16-0 SEC record. How many years had it been since another team finished perfect in the SEC?
   a) 10
   b) 20
   c) 30
   d) 40

ANSWERS 86-100

A86: B. 22-8.

A87: B. UCLA. Coach John Wooden announced his retirement before the game.

A88: B. Mississippi State.

A89: A. Wisconsin.

A90: C. 23,000 seats.

A91: D. $55 million.

A92: Rick Robey.

A93: It was "Adolph Rupp Night" and Rupp passed away as the game was played in Allen Field House on Naismith Drive in Lawrence, Kansas.

A94: Goose.

A95: D. 24.

A96: C. 23.

A97: Kentucky's win over Auburn gave the Wildcats the best record in the SEC but more importantly it ended U.K.'s two-year probation.

A98: Michigan beat Kentucky 81-78 in overtime to advance to the championship game. This was Mashburn's last game as a Wildcat.

A99: C. 31 points. U.K. outscored LSU 62-27 to record the historic comeback.

A100: D. 40 years. This was also Kentucky's 25th win in a row. That mark tied a school record for most consecutive wins in a single season. The Wildcats added two more wins to establish 27 as the new record.

QUESTIONS 101-110

Q101: On November 20, 1997, new U.K. coach Tubby Smith opened the season with an 88-49 win at Rupp Arena over Morehead State. Name the U.K. All-American who was the coach of the Morehead State Eagles.

Q102: Against what team did Kentucky overcome a 17-point deficit to advance to the 1998 NCAA championship game?

Q103: Wildcat legend Cawood Ledford passed away in his home in Harlan, Kentucky, on September 5, 2001. Why was a Rupp Arena planned tribute to Ledford cancelled?

Q104: The 1,800th win in school history came vs. North Carolina on December 8, 2001. True or False: Kentucky was only the second team in NCAA history to record 1,800 wins.

Q105: On March 16, 2003, U.K. defeated Mississippi State to win its 24th league tournament championship. The Wildcats also finished with a perfect SEC record. How many seasons had it been since an SEC team finished the regular season undefeated and won the conference tournament?
   a) 61
   b) 51
   c) 41
   d) 31

Q106: Who scored 54 points to break Dan Issel's 39-year-old school record of 53 points in a game?

Q107: What team did the Wildcats defeat in front of a Rupp Arena record-setting crowd of 24,479 fans on January 2, 2010?

Q108: What team knocked U.K. out of the 2011 Final Four when they beat the Wildcats 56-55?

Q109: What was significant about Kentucky's 108-58 season opening win over Marist on November 11, 2011?

Q110: On January 29, 2013, Nerlens Noel set a school record for blocked shots. How many Ole Miss shots did Noel block?
   a) 11
   b) 12
   c) 13
   d) 14

ANSWERS 101-110

A101: Kyle Macy.

A102: Duke. U.K. defeated Duke 86-84.

A103: Ledford's tribute was cancelled after the 9/11 terrorist attacks.

A104: False. Kentucky became the first team to record 1,800 wins.

A105: B. 51.

A106: Jodie Meeks. Meeks also sank ten three-pointers, breaking Tony Delk's team record of nine three-pointers.

A107: University of Louisville.

A108: University of Connecticut knocked Kentucky out of the Final Four. The UConn Huskies went on to win the 2011 NCAA championship.

A109: Kentucky's season opening win over Marist was its record-setting 34th consecutive win at Rupp Arena.

A110: B. 12 blocked shots. Amazingly, Noel picked up his fourth foul with 9:52 left in the second half but still came up with several key blocks in the final minutes of the game.

"I know I have plenty of enemies, but I'd rather be the most hated winning coach in the country than the most popular losing one."
— Adolph Rupp

4 THE LEGENDS

We know Kentucky basketball legends by their first names, last names, nicknames and jersey numbers. We seem to love them just a little bit more when they are from our home state or better yet when they grew up in a county that we call home. Their jerseys have been retired and hang in Rupp Arena. Some legends have been enshrined and immortalized in the Naismith Hall of Fame in Springfield, Massachusetts. The legends' statistics and records stand alone. Some of their shots were heard around the world while some of their dunks and other moments of glory still generate thousands of views on YouTube and ESPN highlights. Their legacy lives on today when we remember the wins and thrills they gave us when we were all just a little younger than what we are today.

QUESTIONS 111-125

Q111: In 1992, U.K. athletic director C.M. Newton said, "Today, our program is back on top, due largely to four young men who persevered, who weathered the hard times, and who brought the good times back to Kentucky basketball. Their contributions to U.K. basketball cannot be measured in statistics or record books." Name these four seniors who are considered to be the heart and soul of the University of Kentucky basketball program's resurgence.

Q112: Name the 1940 captain and All-SEC guard who became the first Wildcat to have his jersey retired.

Q113: How does the University of Kentucky honor players whose jerseys are retired?

Q114: Name Coach Rupp's "Fabulous Five" players whose jerseys were retired after the 1949 season.

Q115: True or False: When a Kentucky player's jersey is retired, players can no longer wear that number.

Q116: Name the cherished and loyal equipment manager who became one of the few non-playing Wildcats to have his jersey retired.

Q117: Another non-playing Wildcat whose jersey was retired was known as the "Voice of the Wildcats". Name this legendary Wildcat.

Q118: Coach Rupp's 1943-44 team featured a very young roster. Rupp said coaching them was like teaching a kindergarten classroom. Rupp referred to them as "Beardless Wonders". Why did this team consist of fifteen freshmen and two sophomores?

Q119: Name the member of Rupp's 1943-44 "Wildkittens" who became the youngest ever All-American after averaging 12.1 points per game.

Q120: What number game did the 1947-48 "Fabulous Five" first come together as starters?
   a) 10th
   b) 12th
   c) 13th
   d) 16th

Q121: What made Kenny Rollins, Cliff Barker and Alex Groza, three of the "Fabulous Five," so tough?

Q122: Coach Rupp's 1957-58 national champions were known as "The Fiddlin' Five" because Rupp said that they "fiddle and fiddle around" before finally pulling out their wins. Rupp also said, "They might be pretty good barnyard fiddlers, but we have a Carnegie Hall schedule, and it will take violinists to play that competition." Name the "Fiddlin' Five" players.

Q123: The 1965-66 Kentucky Wildcats were known as "Rupp's Runts." How tall was the tallest member of the starting five?

Q124: "Rupp's Runts" finished their season 27-2 and were known for their:
   a) Shooting
   b) Hustle
   c) Passing
   d) Unselfish attitude
   e) All of the above

Q125: True or False: Although "Rupp's Runts" lost the title game to Texas Western, they remain one of the most beloved U.K. basketball teams of all-time.

ANSWERS 111-125

A111: Seniors Sean Woods, John Pelphrey, Deron Feldhaus and Richie Farmer.

A112: Layton "Mickey" Rouse.

A113: Retired jersey recipients are presented with a framed jersey and are also honored with a banner that is displayed at Rupp Arena.

A114: Cliff Barker, Ralph Beard, Alex Groza, "Wah Wah" Jones and Kenny Rollins.

A115: False. U.K. players can wear retired numbers because the NCAA Rules Committee limited the numbers that players can wear.

A116: Bill "Mr. Wildcat" Keightley.

A117: Broadcasting legend Cawood Ledford's jersey was retired. Ledford is known as "The Voice of the Wildcats".

A118: This Wildcat team finished 19-2 and was so youthful because other players had left to serve in World War II.

A119: Bob Brannum became the youngest ever All-American. He was 17.

A120: B. 12th game.

A121: Kenny Rollins, Cliff Barker and Alex Groza were World War II veterans. They were in their early to late twenties. Barker had spent 16 months in a German prisoner of war camp. While in prison Barker practiced dribbling by using a volleyball that was provided to him by the Red Cross. Barker also lost two teeth after a German soldier hit him with a rifle butt.

A122: Johnny Cox, John Crigler, Adrian Smith, Vernon Hatton and Ed Beck. After the Wildcats won the 1958 national championship, Rupp said, "Those boys are certainly not concert violinists, but they sure can fiddle."

A123: Both guard Tommy Kron and center Thad Jaracz were the tallest members of "Rupp's Runts" starting five players. Kron and Jaracz were 6' 5".

A124: E. All of the above.

A125: True. The renowned "Rupp's Runts" were honored during the 1990-91 season, commemorating the 25th anniversary of their remarkable season.

QUESTIONS 126-140

Q126: Name this member of "Rupp's Runts" who led the team in points and rebounds and was known for his speed, quickness, agility and jumping skills.

Q127: Name this 1928-30 Wildcat All-American who later became an assistant for Coach Rupp.

Q128: This two-time All-American was named the 1933 Helms Athletic Foundation National College Player of the Year.
   a) Aggie Sale
   b) Evan Settle
   c) Crittenden Blair
   d) George Yates

Q129: This Ashland, Kentucky, native played four sports at U.K. and was a starter on Coach Rupp's first team. He also earned All-American recognition in 1933.
   a) Ralph Kercheval
   b) Bill Davis
   c) Ellis Johnson
   d) Dave Lawrence

Q130: True or False: All-American and Helms Athletic Foundation National College Player of the Year Leroy Edwards was a four-year starter.

Q131: Which of the following is NOT one of Leroy Edwards' nicknames?
   a) "Cowboy"
   b) "Big Ed"
   c) "Wonder Boy"
   d) "Big Boy"

Q132: Name the legend who earned All-American honors in 1941 and is remembered for his backcourt skills.
   a) Lee Huber
   b) Mel Brewer
   c) Milt Ticco
   d) Jim Jordan

Q133: Who recruited New York City native Bernie Opper to come to U.K.?

Q134: Name the Wildcat legend who led his high school in Harlan, Kentucky, to runners-up in the 1942 state championship.

Q135: This legend known for his toughness left U.K. in 1949 as the all-time leading Wildcat scorer with 1,744 points. He was also a three-time All-American and a two-time NCAA Tournament Most Valuable Player.

Q136: Who sank the clutch late free throw to lift U.K. over Rhode Island 46-45 in the 1946 NIT championship in Madison Square Garden?
a) Ralph Beard
b) Jack Tingle
c) "Wah Wah" Jones
d) Jack Parkinson

Q137: True or False: Five Wildcats were named to the 1947 SEC All-Tournament First Team.

Q138: It was once said that this player could do anything with a basketball except make it talk.
a) Ralph Beard
b) Cliff Barker
c) "Wah Wah" Jones
d) Alex Groza

Q139: In addition to ordering the seven-foot tall and skinny Bill Spivey to eat extra meals each day, assistant coach Harry Lancaster also insisted that Spivey should do what?

Q140: How many points did Georgia native Spivey average for U.K.'s 1951 NCAA championship team?
a) 16.3
b) 17.1
c) 18.7
d) 19.2

ANSWERS 126-140

A126: Pat Riley.

A127: Paul McBrayer.

A128: A. Aggie Sale.

A129: C. Ellis Johnson.

A130: False. Leroy Edwards played only one season for U.K.

A131: C. "Wonder Boy".

A132: A. Lee Huber.

A133: Himself. Bernie Opper decided to attend Kentucky after watching the Wildcats play in Madison Square Garden.

A134: Wallace "Wah Wah" Jones.

A135: Alex Groza.

A136: A. Freshman Ralph Beard sank the clutch NIT championship-winning free throw.

A137: True. "Wah Wah" Jones, Jack Tingle, Joe Holland, Ralph Beard and Kenny Rollins were all named to the 1947 SEC All-Tournament First Team.

A138: B. Cliff Barker.

A139: Assistant coach Harry Lancaster insisted Bill Spivey drink several milkshakes each day.

A140: D. 19.2 points.

QUESTIONS 141-155

Q141: What three Western Kentucky natives enjoyed defeating Ole Miss 86-39 in Owensboro in front of their hometown fans during the 1950-51 season?

Q142: What kind of shot was Cliff Hagan known for?

Q143: How many points did Cliff Hagan score against Temple in the 1953-54 season opener?
   a) 43
   b) 46
   c) 48
   d) 51

Q144: Who became the first junior college transfer to play for Adolph Rupp?
   a) Sonny Corum
   b) Bob Burrow
   c) Billy Evans
   d) John Brewer

Q145: Who was the second Wildcat to score 50 points in a game when he helped the Wildcats defeat LSU 107-65 during the 1955-56 season?

Q146: Who is the Hazard, Kentucky, Wildcat who led his high school team to a 1955 state championship?

Q147: Who is the Kentucky player who led the 1960-61 team in rebounding and finished second in scoring in his only season with U.K.?

Q148: Whose last-second jumper lifted U.K. over Duke 81-79 in the championship game of the 1963 Sugar Bowl Tournament? After the win, the Wildcats earned a number one ranking in the polls for the first time since 1953.
   a) Pat Riley
   b) Cotton Nash
   c) Larry Conley
   d) Terry Mobley

Q149: Name the Ashland, Kentucky, native—and son of a coach—whose basketball intelligence and passing skills are considered by many as the sharpest in U.K. history.

Q150: Cotton Nash scored 1,770 career points to surpass Alex Groza's all-time U.K. record. How many points and rebounds did Nash average in his last Kentucky season?

a) 23 points, 10.4 rebounds
b) 23.6 points, 11 rebounds
c) 24 points, 11.7 rebounds
d) 25 points, 9.8 rebounds

Q151: True or False: Cotton Nash remains the only Kentucky player to have ever averaged 20 or more points for three seasons.

Q152: True or False: Nash's career average of 22.7 points per game is the highest in Kentucky basketball history.

Q153: What native of Owensboro, Kentucky, joined Pat Riley and Louie Dampier in the 1964-65 recruiting class? HINT: His son became a U.K. legend and NBA star.

Q154: Name U.K.'s assistant coach whose fierce off-season conditioning program is credited as a primary reason "Rupp's Runts" became one of the best U.K. teams in history.

Q155: Pat Riley and Harry Lancaster stated these two lesser known "Rupp's Runts" were the real MVP's of the team because of their unselfish play and sacrifices for the good of the team

ANSWERS 141-155

A141: Frank Ramsey, Bobby Watson and Cliff Hagan.

A142: Hook shot.

A143: D. 51.

A144: B. Bob Burrow.

A145: Bob Burrow.

A146: Johnny Cox. Cox was known for his jumpers, hook shots and superb rebounding skills.

A147: Roger Newman.

A148: D. Terry Mobley.

A149: Larry Conley.

A150: C. 24 points, 11.7 rebounds.

A151: True. Nash's career average was 22.7 points per game.

A152: False. Dan Issel's career average was 25.8 points per game.

A153: 6' 6" Wayne Chapman. Rex Chapman is his son.

A154: Joe B. Hall.

A155: Tommy Kron and Larry Conley.

QUESTIONS 156-170

Q156: This U.K. legend was known for sinking long range jump shots. He later became the all-time leading scorer in the old ABA (American Basketball Association).

Q157: How many points did the legendary trio of Mike Casey, Dan Issel and Mike Pratt combine to score for Kentucky?
a) 4,678
b) 4,783
c) 4,844
d) 5,032

Q158: This Wildcat earned a starting backcourt spot as a sophomore and then averaged double-digit points in his final two years.
a) Phil Argento
b) Thad Jaracz
c) Larry Conley
d) Gene Stewart

Q159: True or False: Dan Issel left U.K. as its all-time leading scorer and second best all-time rebounder.

Q160: Mike Casey's injury during the 1969-70 season is said to have cost Kentucky another NCAA championship. How was Casey injured?

Q161: True or False: After Tom Payne broke the racial barrier, U.K. secured other black Kentucky high school talents such as Wes Unseld, Clem Haskins, Butch Beard, Mike Redd, Jerome Perry, Jim McDaniels, Jim Rose and brothers Dwight and Greg Smith.

Q162: How tall was Tom Payne?

Q163: This Wildcat scored 13 points off the bench in his final home game … and his son would later become one of U.K.'s best outside shooters.

Q164: This lefty legend was a remarkable shooter. He averaged 15.5 points per game during his three Kentucky seasons.

Q165: This sophomore averaged 18.7 points per game and turned in a season-high 40-point performance vs. Georgia.

Q166: This 1974-75 Wildcat made 15 of 21 field goals and scored 35 points in a crucial come-from-behind win over North Carolina.

Q167: What was extra special about Mike Flynn's 22-point game that led

Kentucky over the Indiana Hoosiers 92-90 in the 1975 Mideast Regional?

Q168: The 1975-76 Wildcats started the season 10-10. How did they perform in their final ten games?
   a) 10-0
   b) 9-1
   c) 8-2
   d) 7-3

Q169: Name the high-flyin' Wildcat who electrified fans with his dunks. HINT: His nickname was "Jammin".

Q170: Name the four Wildcats who put U.K. basketball back on top after compiling a 102-21 record together with two NCAA championship games, one national title and an NIT championship.

ANSWERS 156-170

A156: Louie Dampier.

A157: D. 5,032 points.

A158: A. Phil Argento.

A159: False. Dan Issel left U.K. as the all-time leading scorer and rebounder.

A160: Automobile accident.

A161: False. U.K. continued to pass on many talented black Kentucky high school players.

A162: 7' 2".

A163: Terry Mills. His son Cameron played for Kentucky 25 years later.

A164: Tom Parker.

A165: Kevin Grevey.

A166: Jimmy Dan Conner.

A167: Mike Flynn was Indiana's "Mr. Basketball" in 1971.

A168: A. 10-0. U.K. won its last ten games of the season to win the 1976 NIT championship.

A169: "Jammin" James Lee.

A170: Jack Givens, Rick Robey, Mike Phillips and James Lee.

QUESTIONS 171-185

Q171: What nickname did Cawood Ledford give Dwight Anderson because of his remarkable athleticism and tenacious play?

Q172: Who scored 84 points in the 1979 SEC Tournament? His 25 points led U.K. past Alabama 101-100 in the quarterfinals.
a) Kyle Macy
b) James Lee
c) Truman Claytor
d) Rick Robey

Q173: What 7' 1" Wildcat legend was known for running like a guard and for his ability to hit the medium-range jumper?

Q174: Charles Hurt was an outstanding rebounder and defender, but his shooting percentage was extraordinary. What was his field goal percentage?
a) 54.2
b) 56.4
c) 59.3
d) 60.2

Q175: Who emerged as a scoring threat when he stepped in for an injured Sam Bowie?
a) Dirk Minniefield
b) Melvin Turpin
c) Derrick Hord
d) Jim Master

Q176: This junior led the Wildcats in scoring during the 1981-82 season with 16.3 points per game.
a) Dirk Minniefield
b) Melvin Turpin
c) Derrick Hord
d) Jim Master

Q177: Who hit a last-second shot to tie the Louisville Cardinals 62-62 and send the 1983 Mideast Regional Final "Dream Game" into overtime?
a) Dirk Minniefield
b) Melvin Turpin
c) Derrick Hord
d) Jim Master

Q178: How many years did Sam Bowie miss before he returned to lead the

Wildcats to the 1984 Final Four?

Q179: True or False: Kentucky dominated "Dream Game II" and easily defeated the Louisville Cardinals.

Q180: The 1983-84 Wildcats were ranked number two in the nation when they went to Kansas and gave the Jayhawks their third worst beating of all-time. What was the final score of that game?
  a) 70-48
  b) 72-50
  c) 73-53
  d) 75-55

Q181: This Wildcat scored five points in the final 43 seconds to help Kentucky defeat Illinois 54-51 in the 1984 Elite Eight game.
  a) Winston Bennett
  b) Dicky Beal
  c) James Blackmon
  d) Sam Bowie

Q182: Name the All-American Wildcat who helped coach Eddie Sutton's first U.K. team finish 32-4.

Q183: This Wildcat was known for hitting last-second clutch shots. HINT: He once hit a 22-foot jumper with eight seconds left in a 61-58 win over LSU.

Q184: Rex Chapman's incredible vertical leap, keen passing ability, fearlessness and toughness made him one of the most celebrated recruits in U.K. history. His popularity was unmatched even before he stepped foot in Rupp Arena. What two nicknames did Chapman have before he even played his first U.K. game?

Q185: What NBA legend made a personal pitch to Rex Chapman in hopes of persuading Chapman to attend his alma mater instead of U.K.?

ANSWERS 171-185

A171: "The Blur".

A172: C. Truman Claytor.

A173: Sam Bowie.

A174: C. 59.3.

A175: B. Melvin Turpin.

A176: C. Derrick Hord.

A177: D. Jim Master. Louisville's press proved too much for U.K. The Cardinals won 80-68.

A178: Two years.

A179: True. U.K. beat U.L. 65-44 and at one point led 55-26.

A180: B. 72-50.

A181: B. Dicky Beal. Beal was voted the Mideast Regional's MVP.

A182: Kenny Walker.

A183: Roger Harden.

A184: "Boy King" and "King Rex". One sportswriter suggested that Lexington should change its name to Rexington.

A185: Michael Jordan. Jordan tried to convince Rex Chapman to become a North Carolina Tar Heel.

QUESTIONS 186-200

Q186: Where did Rex Chapman earn high school All-American honors?

Q187: Against which team did the freshman Chapman score 26 points to lead U.K. to victory 85-51 in front of a national television audience?

Q188: What NBA team selected Rex Chapman with its first draft pick in franchise history?

Q189: Chapman led the Wildcats in scoring his freshman year with 16 points per game. Who was the last Wildcat freshman to lead the team in scoring?

Q190: The 1987-88 Wildcats won their first ten games earning the nation's number one ranking. They beat Indiana in Indianapolis in overtime, and beat Louisville 76-75 with a last-second tip-in at Rupp Arena. What Wildcat tipped in the game-winner?
  a) Eric Manuel
  b) Rex Chapman
  c) Cedric Jenkins
  d) Reggie Hanson

Q191: What U.K. legend teamed with Rex Chapman to form not only one of the best backcourt duos in U.K. history but also one of the best in college basketball history?

Q192: Coach Rick Pitino took over the troubled Wildcats in 1989. Cawood Ledford predicted the Wildcats would win eight games and said if they won ten games then Pitino should earn national Coach of the Year honors. How many games did U.K. win that season?
  a) 8
  b) 10
  c) 12
  d) 14

Q193: Who was the first U.K. player to score 40 points at Rupp Arena?
  a) Derrick Miller
  b) Sean Woods
  c) Jeff Brassow
  d) Richie Farmer

Q194: Name the 6' 8" five-star recruit who chose U.K. despite the program's rocky status and helped lead the 1990-91 Wildcats.
  a) Tony Delk

b) Ron Mercer
c) Jamal Mashburn
d) Derek Anderson

Q195: What coaching legend was Rick Pitino's assistant from 1989-94?

Q196: What high school legend from Clay County emerged as an important leader for Pitino?

Q197: This Wildcat legend was known for his intelligence and basketball instincts and ended his career with 1,257 points.
a) Kyle Macy
b) Deron Feldhaus
c) Walter McCarty
d) John Pelphrey

Q198: Which of the 1992-93 top recruits once scored 70 points in a high school basketball game?
a) Walter McCarty
b) Jared Prickett
c) Rodney Dent
d) Tony Delk

Q199: This high school All-American and top recruit played for coach Bob Hurley at St. Anthony's High School in Jersey City, N.J., but he did not remain a Wildcat long enough for U.K.'s national championship.

Q200: This gritty player tipped in a game-winning buzzer beater to lift the Wildcats over an undefeated Arizona team in the 1993 Maui Classic championship game.

ANSWERS 186-200

A186: Apollo High School in Owensboro, Kentucky.

A187: University of Louisville. Chapman thrilled viewers with his dunks, finger rolls and 5 of 8 three-point shooting—including two from beyond the NBA three-point range of 23' 9". Some consider Chapman's performance against the Cardinals as one of U.K.'s all-time greatest.

A188: Charlotte Hornets.

A189: Alex Groza.

A190: C. Cedric Jenkins.

A191: Ed Davender. Some consider Davender to be the most underappreciated player in U.K. history. He scored 1,637 points, dished out 436 assists and picked 191 steals during his career.

A192: D. 14.

A193: A. Derrick Miller. Miller poured in 40 points on 15 for 28 shooting vs. Vanderbilt to pace a 100-73 shellacking on February 7, 1990. In that same game, Miller also became the 36th player in school history to surpass 1,000 career points.

A194: C. Jamal Mashburn.

A195: Billy Donovan. As Kentucky's assistant coach, Donovan played in the team's preseason scrimmages. Donovan went on to win two national championships as Florida's head coach. He is currently head coach for the Oklahoma City Thunder in the NBA.

A196: Richie Farmer.

A197: D. John Pelphrey.

A198: D. Tony Delk.

A199: Rodrick Rhodes.

A200: Jeff Brassow.

QUESTIONS 201-215

Q201: This Wildcat legend is best known for his steady rebounding and defending skills. He came up one basket short of joining U.K.'s 1,000 point club.

Q202: Which of the following Wildcats did NOT join the 1994-95 squad?
a) Antoine Walker
b) Allen Edwards
c) Scott Padgett
d) Terry Mills
e) Mark Pope

Q203: Louisville native Derek Anderson chose U.K. but was not eligible to play on the 1994-95 team. Why did Anderson have to wait a year before he could become a Wildcat?

Q204: True or False: The super talented Antoine Walker was known for his cool, quiet demeanor both on and off the court.

Q205: What 1996 national champion Wildcat led the team as point guard?

Q206: Tony Delk poured in 30 points as the 1995-96 championship squad trounced Louisville 89-66 at Rupp Arena on the same day this future Wildcat legend committed to U.K. However ... this future legend committed to *football*. Name this All-American.

Q207: U.K. dominated Virginia Tech 84-60 in the 1996 NCAA Tournament second round game. Kentucky's defense held Virginia Tech to ten field goals in the second half. How many dunks did the Wildcats record in the second half?
a) 7
b) 8
c) 9
d) 10

Q208: How many of the 1996 champion Wildcats scored in their Sweet Sixteen pounding of the 12th-ranked Utah Utes?

Q209: These four 1996 national champion Wildcats combined to contribute over 50% of Kentucky's scoring and rebounding ... but did not return for the 1996-97 season.

Q210: Who shot an astounding 63% from behind the three-point line during the 1997 NCAA Tournament and led the Wildcats to their second straight NCAA title game?

Q211: This 1998 NCAA champion led the team in scoring and rebounding and was named SEC Tournament MVP despite a dismal 0 for 18 start from beyond the three-point line.

Q212: This legendary guard played in three Final Fours, won three SEC championships and two NCAA titles.

Q213: Who averaged 12.5 points per game and earned SEC All-Freshman honors during the 1999-2000 season?

Q214: This Wildcat earned both 2000-01 SEC Player of the Year and SEC Tournament MVP honors.

Q215: This lefty legend from Cincinnati sank 57% of his field goal attempts during his first season with the Wildcats.

ANSWERS 201-215

A201: Jared Prickett.

A202: D. Terry Mills. Mills played for the Wildcats from 1968-71. However, his son, Cameron Mills, won a walk-on spot with the Wildcats 1994-95 team.

A203: Derek Anderson had to wait a year before playing for U.K. because he transferred from Ohio State.

A204: False. Walker was a confident, cocky player who seemed to thrive in the spotlight.

A205: C. Anthony Epps from Lebanon, KY, emerged as point guard for the 1996 NCAA champion Wildcats.

A206: Tim Couch.

A207: C. Nine.

A208: 12 Wildcats scored.

A209: Tony Delk, Walter McCarty and Mark Pope were all seniors—plus NBA draft pick Antoine Walker did not return.

A210: Cameron Mills shot 63% from beyond the three-point line during the 1997 NCAA Tournament.

A211: Scott Padgett.

A212: Wayne Turner.

A213: Keith Bogans.

A214: Tayshaun Prince. Prince later earned All-American status for his final season with U.K.

A215: Erik Daniels.

QUESTIONS 216-225

Q216: Keith Bogans ended his Wildcat career with 1,923 points. Where did this rank Bogans in U.K. basketball history?
   a) 3rd best
   b) 4th best
   c) 5th best
   d) 6th best

Q217: Name the three 2003-04 seniors who combined to score 3,283 career points for the Wildcats.

Q218: The 2005 Elite Eight was an epic battle vs. Michigan State that the Wildcats eventually lost 94-88 in double overtime. In that game, who had a buzzer beater bounce on the rim four times before finally dropping to tie the Spartans 75-75?

Q219: A number of special events marked the fortieth anniversary of "Rupp's Runts" in 2005-06. Members of that legendary team were on hand for a match-up vs. South Carolina that ended in spectacular fashion. Who nailed a last-second three-pointer to lift U.K. to a thrilling 80-78 victory with the original "Rupp's Runts" cheering him on?

Q220: What freshman hit four three-pointers to lift the 2006-07 Wildcats over Rick Pitino's Louisville squad?

Q221: This five-star, coach Billy Gillispie recruit from West Virginia was known for both his play and his poised, classy personality.

Q222: This 2007-08 Kentucky player earned both All-SEC first team and All-Defensive team honors.

Q223: On January 13, 2009, Jodie Meeks sank 10 of 15 three-pointers and made 14 of 14 free throws on his way to a school record 54 points—and he did it in front of a national TV audience on ESPN. Which SEC opponent did Meeks embarrass that night?
   a) Florida
   b) Georgia
   c) Arkansas
   d) Tennessee

Q224: Jodie Meeks and Patrick Patterson proved to be one of the best one-two punches in U.K. basketball history. True or False: In 2008-09, they combined to score more than half of the team's total points.

Q225: Meeks earned both All-America and All-SEC honors his final season before entering the NBA draft. How many points per game did he average his final season with Kentucky?

  a) 18.5
  b) 21
  c) 23.7
  d) 24.1

ANSWERS 216-225

A216: B. Fourth best.

A217: Erik Daniels, Gerald Fitch and Cliff Hawkins.

A218: Patrick Sparks. Sparks is recognized as one of the most tenacious and clutch Wildcats of all-time.

A219: Rajon Rondo.

A220: Jodie Meeks. Meeks also won SEC Freshman of the Week honors three times.

A221: Patrick Patterson.

A222: Ramel Bradley was named to the 2007-08 SEC All-Defensive Team.

A223: D. Tennessee.

A224: True.

A225: C. 23.7 points.

"We're chasing greatness."
— John Calipari

5 THE CALIPARI ERA

On April 1, 2009, one of the winningest coaches in NCAA history signed an eight-year $31.65 million (not including incentives) contract to become Big Blue Nation's next head coach. Coach Cal's charisma, tenacity for signing the top recruits, and ability to embrace and shine in the limelight made restoring Kentucky Basketball to its old glory look easy. Although these first seven seasons with Coach Calipari have been nothing short of mesmerizing, fans cannot help but think the best is still yet to come for Cal's Cats.

After leading the 2013-14 Cats to the school's 16th NCAA Final Four, Coach Calipari's efforts were rewarded with a new seven-year contract. Mitch Barnhart, U.K.'s Director of Athletics, stated, "Basketball has long been the marquee sport at the University of Kentucky. It's a sport that the traditions of this university and this state have been founded on. They were developed and sort of started from the get-go by Adolph Rupp and through many good people since. What Cal has done is returned us to those glory days of Final Fours and championship efforts, great players ..." U.K. President Eli Capilouto added, "Under Coach Cal's leadership, the most storied program in NCAA basketball has reached new heights of success and excellence."

In his 23 seasons as a head coach, Calipari has helped 38 of his players fulfill their dreams of playing in the NBA. While coaching at Kentucky, Calipari has helped 25 Wildcats to be selected in the NBA draft. Three have been number one overall picks, ten have been top-five selections, and thirteen have been lottery picks.

In spring 2015, Coach Calipari was elected into the Naismith Memorial Basketball Hall of Fame—and his contract was extended again. His current contract is good through the 2021-22 season. This is great news for Cats fans!

QUESTIONS 226-240

Q226: This Wildcat could have easily entered the NBA draft but chose to come back for his junior season to be a steady, unselfish leader on Coach Calipari's first Kentucky team.

Q227: Name the first two high school All-American recruits who committed to Calipari's first recruiting class.

Q228: Name the top recruit who committed to Coach Cal's first team and also earned Kentucky's "Mr. Basketball" honors.

Q229: Name the starting five Wildcats for the first game of "The Calipari Era".

Q230: The 2009-10 Kentucky team started 19-0 but had to battle through some nail biters. They beat Miami (Ohio) 72-70 on a John Wall 15-footer at the buzzer. They also managed a close win over tenth ranked North Carolina despite a first half 28-2 run and a halftime score of 43-28. What was the final score of this Wildcat win over the Tar Heels at Rupp Arena?
  a) 68-66
  b) 71-70
  c) 74-72
  d) 78-75

Q231: Whose record did John Wall break when he dished out 16 assists in a Wildcat win over Hartford in December 2009?

Q232: How many points and rebounds did DeMarcus Cousins contribute in Kentucky's 71-62 win over rival Louisville in January 2010?

Q233: In March 2010, John Wall led U.K. past Mississippi State in overtime 75-74 to win the SEC Tournament. How many of his 15 points did John Wall score in overtime?
  a) 6
  b) 7
  c) 8
  d) 9

Q234: The 2009-10 Wildcats won 30 games for the 12th time in school history and the first time since going 32-4 in 2003. This was the seventh time a Calipari-coached team won 30 or more games. True or False: This was the fifth consecutive season Coach Calipari coached his team to a 30-win season.

Q235: Name the two teams the number two ranked and number one seeded Wildcats blasted past in the first two rounds of the 2010 NCAA Tournament.

Q236: Tony Delk led U.K. to victory vs. Syracuse in the 1996 championship game with an NCAA Tournament record seven three-pointers. What Wildcat broke this record with eight three-pointers in a 2010 NCAA match-up?

Q237: The 2010 Wildcats beat Cornell University in the 2010 Sweet Sixteen but lost in the Elite Eight game. Name the team and coach that prevented Calipari's first Cats team from advancing to the Final Four.

Q238: After Wall, Cousins, Patterson, Bledsoe and Orton heard their names called in the NBA draft, the Calipari "one and done" era began. Name the two All-American recruits who signed on to play for Calipari in 2010-11.

Q239: Top Calipari recruit Enes Kanter was ruled ineligible and never played a game for the Wildcats. Why was this 6' 11" superstar from Turkey declared permanently ineligible?

Q240: Name the three Wildcat veterans who led the 2010-11 Calipari team to a Final Four.

ANSWERS 226-240

A226: Patrick Patterson.

A227: John Wall and DeMarcus Cousins.

A228: Jon Hood.

A229: DeMarcus Cousins, Darius Miller, Eric Bledsoe, Darnell Dodson and Patrick Patterson. John Wall did not play in the first game of the Coach Calipari era.

A230: A. 68-66.

A231: Travis Ford.

A232: Cousins scored 18 points and grabbed 18 rebounds to help snap Louisville's two-game winning streak between the in-state rivals.

A233: B. Seven.

A234: True.

A235: East Tennessee State 100-71 and Wake Forrest 90-60.

A236: Eric Bledsoe sank eight three-pointers against East Tennessee State University.

A237: Calipari's friend Bob Huggins coached West Virginia to a 73-66 win over the Wildcats in the Elite Eight. The Wildcats missed their first 20 three-point field goal attempts.

A238: All-Americans Terrence Jones and Brandon Knight. This incredible recruiting class also included Doron Lamb, Eloy Vargas, Stacey Poole and Jessamine County prep legend Jarrod Polson.

A239: Enes Kanter was declared permanently ineligible because he received $33,000 in benefits when he played professional basketball overseas.

A240: Brandon Knight, DeAndre Liggins and fan-favorite Josh Harrellson.

QUESTIONS 241-255

Q241: Name the 2010-11 Wildcat who set a freshman scoring record with 32 points in an 85-60 blowout over Mississippi Valley State.

Q242: A month later, a different Wildcat set yet another freshman scoring record. Name the freshman who scored 35 points against Auburn.

Q243: What team did U.K. defeat in the 2011 SEC Tournament title game to claim its 27th SEC championship?

Q244: The 2010-11 Wildcats were given a number four seed in the NCAA Tournament. After sneaking past a pesky Princeton team, the Wildcats pulled off three wins over incredibly tough teams to advance to the Final Four. Name the three powerhouses that U.K. beat.

Q245: Big Blue Nation was thrilled to have the 2010-11 team in the Final Four! When was the last time the Wildcats were in a Final Four?

Q246: The University of Connecticut Huskies defeated the Wildcats in the Final Four match-up. What was the final score?

Q247: Although Wildcats fans were sad to lose Brandon Knight, DeAndre Liggins and Josh Harrellson, they were excited about more Calipari top recruits arriving soon. Name the "Next Cats" who helped make U.K. the top 2011 recruiting class.

Q248: What tough team did the 2011-12 Wildcats beat 75-65 in their second game of the season?

Q249: Anthony Davis' stellar performance propelled U.K. past St. John's 81-59. Davis nearly recorded only the second triple-double in Kentucky history. How many points, rebounds and blocks did Davis record?

Q250: A key leader for the 2012 NCAA national champion Wildcats was 6' 8" senior Darius Miller. Name the Kentucky county Miller is from.

Q251: An overflow Rupp Arena crowd saw the Kentucky Wildcats defeat Roy Williams and the North Carolina Tar Heels 73-72 on December 3, 2011. How many fans saw Anthony Davis rip down a last-second blocked shot to secure this big Big Blue Nation win?
a) 23,788
b) 23,956
c) 24,398
d) 24,532

Q252: The Wildcats flexed their muscle in a masterfully played 74-50 win over LSU. How many points did pre-season SEC Player of the Year and sophomore superstar Terrence Jones score?

    a) 23
    b) 24
    c) 26
    d) 27

Q253: Michael Kidd-Gilchrist's dominant performance helped the Wildcats defeat Louisville 69-62 on New Year's Eve. Sportswriter John Clay described Kidd-Gilchrist as "Superman." Clay wrote, "He was the one leaping over tall defenders in a single bound for a rebound, flying faster than a speeding bullet up the floor on a fast break, more powerful than a locomotive on a baseline drive through a thicket of defenders." How many points and rebounds did "Superman" record in this Wildcat win over their archrival Cardinals?

Q254: What football coach and program inspired Calipari during the mid-season of the 2011-12 NCAA championship team?

    a) Nick Saban / Alabama
    b) Bear Bryant / Alabama
    c) Lou Holtz / Notre Dame
    d) Vince Lombardi / Green Bay Packers

Q255: On January 21, 2012, Kentucky struggled early in the paint but found a way to beat Alabama 77-71 and remain unbeaten in the SEC. How many one-foot shots did the Wildcats miss in the first half?

    a) 13
    b) 14
    c) 16
    d) 17

ANSWERS 241-255

A241: Doron Lamb.

A242: Terrence Jones scored 35 points coming off the bench to break Lamb's freshman scoring record of 32 points. Lamb's 32 point performance also came off the bench.

A243: Florida Gators.

A244: West Virginia, Ohio State and North Carolina.

A245: 1998.

A246: The University of Connecticut Huskies beat Kentucky 56-55 and went on to beat Butler University to win the 2011 NCAA championship.

A247: Marquis Teague, Anthony Davis, Michael Kidd-Gilchrist and Kyle Wiltjer.

A248: Kansas Jayhawks.

A249: Davis scored 15 points, grabbed 15 rebounds and deflected eight blocked shots.

A250: Mason County.

A251: C. 24,398.

A252: D. 27.

A253: 24 points and 19 rebounds.

A254: A. Nick Saban / Alabama.

A255: B. 14.

QUESTIONS 256-270

Q256: On February 11, 2012, Vanderbilt was beating Kentucky 63-61, but the Wildcats' stellar defense held the Commodores scoreless the rest of the game. How long did U.K.'s defense hold Vanderbilt scoreless down the final stretch?
  a) 3:37
  b) 4:10
  c) 4:59
  d) 5:05

Q257: Kentucky beat Florida 74-59 on March 4, 2012, giving the Wildcats a perfect 16-0 regular season SEC record. True or False: This was the first time an SEC team finished undefeated in the SEC since 1956.

Q258: U.K. beat LSU and Florida to advance to the 2012 SEC Tournament finals. What team beat the Wildcats 71-64 in the championship game, holding the Wildcats' field goal percentage to a measly 35.9%?

Q259: How many of U.K.'s first 12 baskets against the Western Kentucky Hilltoppers were slam dunks in its 2012 NCAA Tournament first round match-up?
  a) 7
  b) 6
  c) 5
  d) 4

Q260: In the second round of the 2012 NCAA Tournament, Iowa State forced U.K. to shoot from the outside. This excellent strategy backfired when the Wildcats got hot from three-point range. How many of the Wildcats' 20 three-point attempts did they make?
  a) 8
  b) 9
  c) 10
  d) 11

Q261: How many of the Wildcats' 37 free throw attempts did they make during their 2012 Sweet Sixteen 102-90 win over the Indiana Hoosiers?
  a) 32
  b) 33
  c) 35
  d) 36

Q262: The Wildcats' 102-90 win over the Hoosiers was the first time a

Kentucky team scored over 100 points in an NCAA Tournament game since 1996. Name the team the Wildcats beat 110-72 in a 1996 NCAA Tournament game.

a) San Jose State
b) Wichita State
c) Indiana State
d) Illinois State

Q263: What Wildcat led Kentucky in scoring with 24 points in its Sweet Sixteen win over Indiana?

a) Anthony Davis
b) Michael Kidd-Gilchrist
c) Terrence Jones
d) Marquis Teague

Q264: In Kentucky's Elite Eight 82-70 win over Baylor, Anthony Davis scored 18 points with 11 rebounds and six blocked shots. In that same game, he also broke the SEC record for blocked shots in a single season. Whose record did Davis surpass? HINT: He's a Mississippi State legend, who recorded 170 blocked shots in back-to-back seasons.

Q265: Kentucky's March 2012 victory vs. Baylor gave the Wildcats 36 wins for only the second time in school history. Name the first U.K. team to record 36 wins.

Q266: What Wildcat scored 17 points in a 10:06 first half stretch to help Kentucky take a commanding first half lead over Baylor?

a) Anthony Davis
b) Michael Kidd-Gilchrist
c) Terrence Jones
d) Marquis Teague

Q267: University of Louisville battled back from a ten-point deficit to tie U.K. at 49-49 in the Final Four state rivalry match-up. However, Anthony Davis' 18 points and 14 rebounds lifted Kentucky to a 69-61 win. Davis also became just the second freshman in school history to record 20 double-doubles. Who was the first?

Q268: What two words did Coach Calipari write down and carry with him onto the floor of the 2012 NCAA championship game against the Kansas Jayhawks?

Q269: Kentucky jumped out to an 18-point lead against Kansas in that title game. What was the Wildcats' field goal percentage in the first half?

a) 48.5%
b) 51%
c) 52%

d) 53.3%

Q270: True or False: Anthony Davis' third blocked shot of the game gave him the NCAA single season record.

ANSWERS 256-270

A256: B. 4:10.

A257: False. This was the third time an SEC team finished the regular season undefeated in league play. The Wildcats finished undefeated in the SEC during the 1995-96 and 2002-03 seasons.

A258: The Vanderbilt Commodores held Kentucky to a 35.9 field goal percentage in the 2012 SEC Tournament title game.

A259: B. Six slam dunks.

A260: C. Ten. Doron Lamb made 5 of 7 three-point attempts.

A261: C. 35.

A262: A. San Jose State.

A263: B. Michael Kidd-Gilchrist.

A264: Jarvis Varnado.

A265: "The Fabulous Five" (1947-48).

A266: B. Michael Kidd-Gilchrist.

A267: DeMarcus Cousins.

A268: "Blue Together".

A269: D. 53.3%.

A270: False. Davis' third blocked shot gave him the NCAA single season record for most blocked shots by a freshman.

QUESTIONS 271-285

Q271: In the 2012 title game vs. Kansas, Anthony Davis grabbed 16 rebounds—giving him 30 rebounds in the Final Four, the most since 1983. Name the basketball legend who grabbed an astounding 40 rebounds in the 1983 Final Four.

Q272: Davis was named the NCAA Tournament Most Outstanding Player. How many other freshmen had earned that honor?
   a) 3
   b) 4
   c) 5
   d) 6

Q273: Kentucky beat Kansas 67-59 in the 2012 title game. What Wildcat led U.K. with 22 points, including clutch back-to-back three-pointers in a crucial second half stretch?
   a) Doron Lamb
   b) Michael Kidd-Gilchrist
   c) Terrence Jones
   d) Marquis Teague

Q274: U.K. dominated the 2012 NCAA Tournament. How many of its 240 minutes of NCAA Tournament basketball did the Wildcats spend trailing their six opponents?
   a) 15 minutes and 17 seconds
   b) 12 minutes and 43 seconds
   c) 10 minutes and 4 seconds
   d) 9 minutes and 6 seconds

Q275: The 2012-13 season proved to be a down year for Calipari's Cats who finished 21-12. However, one highlight from a January 19, 2013, game against Auburn was nominated for the GEICO Play of the Year. Describe this highlight.

Q276: In 2012-13, this Wildcat scored 20 points—including two free throws with one second left on the clock—to lift Kentucky past LSU 75-70.

Q277: In January 2013, this sophomore scored 26 points—including five three-pointers—in an important 87-74 road win over 16th-ranked Mississippi.

Q278: Ole Miss coach Andy Kennedy said Nerlens Noel "was the difference in the game" after Noel's 12 blocked shots set a school record and allowed U.K. to seal the victory. Yet Kentucky coach John Calipari said Noel "played well" but was "struggling for consistency." What part of Noel's game tempered Calipari's enthusiasm?

Q279: Nerlens Noel was leading the nation with 106 blocks when his season ended with an injury. How many blocks per game was he averaging?
   a) 3.8
   b) 4.4
   c) 4.8
   d) 5.1

Q280: What kind of injury ended the 6' 10" freshman Nerlens Noel's season?

Q281: What two 2012-13 Wildcats each scored 19 points in a thrilling 72-68 overtime win against Texas A&M?

Q282: Another highlight for the 2012-13 Kentucky Wildcats was knocking off an 11th-ranked team on Senior Day. Name the team U.K. upset.

Q283: This fifth year senior scored eight overtime points in an impressive 90-83 win over Missouri.

Q284: In 2012-13, this Olathe, Kansas, native earned SEC Freshman of the Week honors ... twice. Name him.

Q285: Kentucky's 2012-13 season came to an end with a NIT first round loss. Name the team that knocked the Wildcats out of the tournament.

ANSWERS 271-285

A271: Hakeem Olajuwon.

A272: A. Three other freshmen had been named NCAA Tournament Most Outstanding Player.

A273: A. Doron Lamb.

A274: D. Nine minutes and six seconds.

A275: Nerlens Noel's monster alley-oop slam dunk against Auburn was nominated for the GEICO Play of the Year.

A276: Alex Poythress. Poythress also grabbed 12 rebounds.

A277: Kyle Wiltjer.

A278: Noel took just one shot from the floor and also missed six of eight free throw attempts.

A279: B. 4.4 blocks per game. Noel also was averaging 10.5 points per game and was ranked second in the SEC for rebounding with 9.5 rebounds per game.

A280: Nerlens Noel tore his ACL.

A281: Julius Mays and Nerlens Noel both scored 19 points against Texas A&M.

A282: Florida.

A283: Julius Mays. Mays finished with 24 points, including 21 second half points.

A284: Willie Cauley-Stein.

A285: Robert Morris.

QUESTIONS 286-300

Q286: In April 2013, three more top recruits committed to Kentucky to solidify Calipari's 2013-14 "Next Cats" recruiting class as the best in the nation. Name these three recruits who joined the already committed Wildcats Aaron Harrison, Andrew Harrison, Marcus Lee, Derek Willis and James Young.

Q287: Name the Richmond, Kentucky, recruit from Madison Central High School who became the 17th Wildcat to boast the Kentucky "Mr. Basketball" title as the state's top prep star.

Q288: How many of Coach Calipari's first five recruiting classes were ranked number one in the nation?
  a) 2
  b) 3
  c) 4
  d) 5

Q289: True or False: Alex Poythress, Jarrod Polson and Patrick Patterson earned degrees in three years.

Q290: True or False: After the spring 2014 semester, the Wildcats' cumulative grade point average (GPA) was 3.11.

Q291: Coach Calipari recorded his 20th consecutive 20-win season when Kentucky finished 2013-14 with a 29-11 record. True or False: Calipari's streak of 20-win seasons was the longest among active coaches.

Q292: Name the 2013-14 Wildcat who steadily averaged 14.3 points per game and finished the season with an impressive 82 three-pointers.
  a) Aaron Harrison
  b) Andrew Harrison
  c) James Young
  d) Julius Randle

Q293: Name the SEC team that swept the 2013-14 Wildcats with two overtime wins.

Q294: What Wildcat hit a game-winning shot with 3.9 seconds left in overtime to lift Kentucky past LSU 77-76?
  a) Aaron Harrison
  b) Andrew Harrison
  c) James Young
  d) Julius Randle

Q295: Name the Kentucky native who earned 2014 SEC Community Service Team honors for visiting sick children at U.K. Children's Hospital and for mentoring kids in need and kids battling terminal illness.

Q296: Julius Randle won the SEC Freshman of the Year award after finishing the regular season with averages of 15.4 points per game and 10.5 rebounds per game. Randle joined Anthony Davis as the first two Wildcats to finish the regular season averaging a double-double since 1985. Name the 1984-85 Wildcat legend who averaged a double-double.

Q297: The 2013-14 Wildcats were the number one ranked team in the preseason poll … but they entered the postseason with only three players with NCAA Tournament experience. Name these three players who had a combined *ten minutes* of NCAA Tournament experience.

Q298: In Kentucky's first round win over Kansas State, Willie Cauley-Stein finished with two points, eight rebounds and four blocks. How many steals did Cauley-Stein record?
a) 5
b) 4
c) 3
d) 2

Q299: Who hit a three-pointer with 1:41 left in the game to put the Wildcats up 73-71 over the Wichita State Shockers in the second round of the 2014 NCAA Tournament?
a) Aaron Harrison
b) Andrew Harrison
c) James Young
d) Julius Randle

Q300: What was Wichita State's 2013-14 season record after Kentucky knocked them out of the NCAA Tournament?

ANSWERS 286-300

A286: Dominique Hawkins, Dakari Johnson and Julius Randle.

A287: Dominique Hawkins.

A288: C. Four.

A289: True.

A290: True.

A291: True.

A292: C. James Young.

A293: Arkansas.

A294: D. Julius Randle.

A295: Jon Hood from Madisonville, Kentucky.

A296: Kenny Walker.

A297: Brian Long, Jon Hood and Jarrod Polson combined for ten minutes of NCAA Tournament experience.

A298: B. Four.

A299: C. James Young.

A300: 35-1.

QUESTIONS 301-315

Q301: Against Wichita State, Julius Randle boasted 13 points, ten rebounds, and a career-best six assists to become the first player since 2003 to record at least ten points, ten rebounds and five assists in an NCAA Tournament game. Name the last player to accomplish this feat and the team he played for.

Q302: In the 2014 Sweet Sixteen match-up of in-state rivals, Kentucky found itself trailing Louisville 18-5 in the first half. What was the score after Aaron Harrison hit a three-pointer with 39 seconds left in the game?
a) 70-68
b) 68-66
c) 71-70
d) 73-71

Q303: What was Louisville's record after U.K. knocked them out of the 2014 NCAA Tournament?
a) 31-6
b) 30-7
c) 29-8
d) 28-9

Q304: Michigan jumped out to an early eight-point lead over Kentucky in the Elite Eight game. Who slammed three dunks in four possessions to cut Michigan's lead to 14-12?
a) Willie Cauley-Stein
b) Marcus Lee
c) Julius Randle
d) Alex Poythress

Q305: True or False: Kentucky trailed Michigan 37-33 at halftime.

Q306: Aaron Harrison's fourth three-pointer vs. Michigan is a shot Wildcats fans will remember for a long time. How many seconds were on the clock when Harrison hit his clutch game-winning shot?
a) 3
b) 4
c) 5
d) 6

Q307: The 2013-14 Wildcats knocked off three Top Ten teams to advance to the Final Four in what many said was the most stacked NCAA bracket of all-time. In addition to beating three Top Ten teams, what else was significant about knocking off Wichita State, Louisville and Michigan?

Q308: Kentucky trailed Wisconsin by eight points early in the Final Four match-up. The Wildcats cut the Badgers' lead to 40-36 at halftime. U.K. went on a 9-0 run early in the second half and later went on another run that matched its longest run of the season. What was that run?
   a) 12-0
   b) 13-0
   c) 14-0
   d) 15-0

Q309: How many seconds were on the clock when Aaron Harrison hit his three-pointer that gave Kentucky a 74-73 lead over Wisconsin?
   a) 2
   b) 3
   c) 5
   d) 6

Q310: U.K.'s 2014 Final Four appearance was the school's third Final Four in four years. Name the last school to accomplish that feat.

Q311: The Kentucky vs. Wisconsin Final Four game set an NCAA Final Four attendance record. How many spectators attended this historic game at AT&T Stadium in Arlington, Texas?
   a) 71,225
   b) 73,479
   c) 75,984
   d) 79,444

Q312: True or False: Kentucky's 2014 Final Four starting line-up against Wisconsin consisted of five freshmen.

Q313: What was Coach Calipari's NCAA Tournament record with Kentucky before losing to the University of Connecticut in the 2014 title game?
   a) 18-2
   b) 17-3
   c) 16-4
   d) 19-1

Q314: After Kentucky beat Wisconsin in the 2014 Final Four, the Wildcats boasted an NCAA Tournament record of 116-46. True or False: Kentucky's 116-46 NCAA Tournament record was the best of all-time.

Q315: True or False: Aaron Harrison started 40 games for the 2013-14 Wildcats and averaged 10.9 points and four assists per game.

ANSWERS 301-315

A301: Dwyane Wade. Wade was a Golden Eagle for Marquette University.

A302: A. 70-68.

A303: A. 31-6.

A304: B. Marcus Lee. Lee scored ten points and secured eight rebounds in 15 minutes of playing time.

A305: False. The halftime score was 37-37. This was the first time Kentucky was tied at halftime in the 2013-14 season.

A306: B. Four.

A307: Louisville, Michigan and Wichita State were all in the 2013 Final Four.

A308: D. 15-0.

A309: D. Six.

A310: UCLA. The Bruins actually earned three consecutive Final Four appearances in 2006, 2007 and 2008.

A311: D. 79,444.

A312: True. U.K.'s starting five freshmen were Aaron Harrison, Andrew Harrison, Dakari Johnson, James Young and Julius Randle.

A313: A. 18-2.

A314: True.

A315: False. Aaron Harrison started 39 of 40 games.

QUESTIONS 316-330

Q316: True or False: During the four games prior to the 2014 NCAA title game, the Wildcats rallied to overcome deficits of nine, 13, ten and nine points.

Q317: True or False: The 2013-14 Wildcats entered the NCAA championship game as an eighth-seeded team.

Q318: UConn beat U.K. in the 2014 NCAA title game. The Huskies jumped out to a 30-15 lead, but the Wildcats managed to close it to 35-31 at halftime. What was the final score?

Q319: A rumor surfaced after the title game that Coach Calipari was going to become the Los Angeles Lakers head coach. How did Calipari respond to reporters when asked if he was going to the Lakers?

Q320: Name the 2013-14 Wildcat who became the fifth Calipari-era player to receive All-American honors.

Q321: Coach Calipari's record at Kentucky was 152-37 after five seasons (through 2013-14). He led U.K. to four Elite Eights, three Final Fours and two national title games. The University of Kentucky decided to extend his contract. How many years was Coach Calipari's contract for?
   a) 5
   b) 6
   c) 7
   d) 8

Q322: The "Next Cats" 2014-15 recruiting class is considered one of the best of all-time. Name the four All-Americans and Jordan Brand Classic players who committed to becoming Wildcats.

Q323: After the 2014-15 Kentucky squad beat Georgia 72-64 to move to 17-0 in the SEC, a fan held up a sign that read, "U.K. The ..." Complete the quote.

Q324: How many turnovers did U.K. commit in the first half of its 72-64 win over Georgia?
   a) 5
   b) 3
   c) 1
   d) 0

Q325: What team did U.K. beat to complete its perfect regular and SEC

season?
a) Missouri
b) Mississippi State
c) Florida
d) LSU

Q326: The 2014-15 Wildcats won 19 home games, breaking the record that was shared by three U.K. teams. Name the three teams that won 18 home games.

Q327: What Wildcat earned SEC Freshman of the Year honors?

Q328: Who scored 18 points to help Kentucky defeat Auburn 91-67 in the SEC Tournament semifinals?
a) Willie Cauley-Stein
b) Trey Lyles
c) Karl-Anthony Towns
d) Marcus Lee

Q329: Kentucky won the 2015 SEC Tournament by beating the 21st-ranked Arkansas Razorbacks. How many SEC titles did this win give U.K.?
a) 26
b) 27
c) 28
d) 29

Q330: Who scored 21 points and grabbed 11 rebounds for the Wildcats in their 2015 NCAA Tournament first round game with Hampton?
a) Willie Cauley-Stein
b) Trey Lyles
c) Karl-Anthony Towns
d) Marcus Lee

ANSWERS 316-330

A316: True.

A317: True.

A318: 60-54.

A319: When asked if he was going to become the Los Angeles Lakers new head coach, Coach Calipari stated, "I got the best job in the country."

A320: Julius Randle.

A321: C. Seven years.

A322: Devin Booker, Karl-Anthony Towns, Trey Lyles and Tyler Ulis.

A323: The fan's sign read "The Unbeatables".

A324: D. Zero.

A325: C. Florida Gators.

A326: The 1985-86, 2009-10 and 2011-12 teams all won 18 home games.

A327: Karl-Anthony Towns.

A328: A. Willie Cauley-Stein.

A329: C. 28.

A330: C. Karl-Anthony Towns.

QUESTIONS 331-345

Q331: Whose nine points, five assists, three steals and three rebounds helped Kentucky defeat Cincinnati in the 2015 NCAA Tournament second round game?
a) Andrew Harrison
b) Trey Lyles
c) Karl-Anthony Towns
d) Tyler Ulis

Q332: Who scored 11 points and grabbed 11 rebounds in Kentucky's win over Cincinnati?
a) Willie Cauley-Stein
b) Trey Lyles
c) Karl-Anthony Towns
d) Marcus Lee

Q333: U.K. dominated West Virginia in the 2015 Sweet Sixteen match-up. What was the final score of this trouncing?
a) 78-39
b) 68-36
c) 73-41
d) 75-43

Q334: West Virginia's point total was the second lowest allowed by a U.K. team in NCAA Tournament history. In what year did a Kentucky team hold Oklahoma A&M to a measly 36 points in an NCAA title game?

Q335: U.K. dominated another game earlier in the season. How badly did the Wildcats beat up on Missouri on January 13, 2015?
a) 73-29
b) 68-30
c) 86-37
d) 81-39

Q336: Kentucky beat a 32-5 Notre Dame team to advance to the 2015 Final Four. U.K. made 10 of 27 field goal attempts in the first half. How many of its 20 second half attempts did they make?
a) 15
b) 14
c) 13
d) 12

Q337: The first half of the 2015 Elite Eight game against Notre Dame

consisted of ten ties and 13 lead changes. Whose tip-in basket at the buzzer tied the game 31-31 at halftime?
a) Willie Cauley-Stein
b) Trey Lyles
c) Karl-Anthony Towns
d) Marcus Lee

Q338: Who scored a career-high 25 points against Notre Dame?
a) Willie Cauley-Stein
b) Trey Lyles
c) Karl-Anthony Towns
d) Marcus Lee

Q339: After Kentucky's 2015 Elite Eight win over Notre Dame, the U.K. defense had held its 2014-15 opponents to a combined field goal percentage of what?
a) 33.3%
b) 35.2%
c) 36.1%
d) 36.8%

Q340: With six seconds left in the Elite Eight game, what U.K. player sank two clutch free throws to break the 66-66 tie and lift the Wildcats over the Fighting Irish?
a) Devin Booker
b) Aaron Harrison
c) Karl-Anthony Towns
d) Andrew Harrison

Q341: Kentucky advanced to the 2015 Final Four and faced a rematch with the University of Wisconsin Badgers. Andrew Harrison drained a three-pointer on the Wildcats' first possession of the game. How many consecutive games with a three-point basket did this give U.K.?
a) 531
b) 679
c) 764
d) 939

Q342: U.K.'s bench outscored Wisconsin's bench 12-8. True or False: Kentucky's bench outscored its opponents' bench in every game in the 2014-15 season.

Q343: The Wildcats went on an 8-0 run with their stellar defense keeping the Badgers scoreless for more than six minutes to grab a 60-56 lead. However, Wisconsin then went on its own run after a Sam Dekker basket. What was the Badgers run that propelled them to a 71-64 upset of "The

Unbeatables"?
   a) 7-0
   b) 8-0
   c) 9-0
   d) 10-0

Q344: By what margin did the Badgers outrebound the Wildcats?
   a) 30-20
   b) 32-24
   c) 34-22
   d) 35-26

Q345: The loss to Wisconsin left the Wildcats with the most disappointing 38-1 record in history. It also left U.K. with an all-time 120-48 record in the NCAA Tournament. True or False: Kentucky's 120 NCAA Tournament wins are the most in NCAA Tournament history.

ANSWERS 331-345

A331: D. Tyler Ulis.

A332: B. Trey Lyles.

A333: A. 78-39.

A334: The 1949 U.K. squad held Oklahoma A&M to 36 points in the national championship game.

A335: C. 86-37.

A336: A. 15. The Wildcats shot a staggering 75% from the field in the second half, including making nine of their last nine shots in the final 10:24 of the game!

A337: B. Trey Lyles.

A338: C. Karl-Anthony Towns.

A339: B. 35.2%.

A340: D. Andrew Harrison.

A341: D. 939 consecutive games with a three-pointer.

A342: False. The Arkansas Razorbacks' bench outscored U.K.'s bench in the SEC title game.

A343: B. 8-0 run.

A344: C. Wisconsin outrebounded Kentucky 34-22.

A345: True.

QUESTIONS 346-360

Q346: Kentucky's 38 wins in 2014-15 tied the highest total by any team in NCAA history. Name the only two other teams to accomplish a 38-win season.

Q347: Coach Calipari's record at U.K. after the 2014-15 season was 190-38 for a .833 winning percentage. True or False: This winning percentage is the best in U.K. coaching history.

Q348: In 2015, Coach Calipari led Kentucky to its fourth Final Four appearance in five years. He was just the third coach in NCAA history to accomplish this feat. Name the other two coaches.

Q349: Willie Cauley-Stein was named one of ten John Wooden All-American finalists. Name the other former Wildcat who was one of the ten 2015 finalists.

Q350: Willie Cauley-Stein was named a consensus First Team All-American. How many First Team All-Americans has U.K. had in school history?
   a) 22
   b) 23
   c) 24
   d) 25

Q351: How many games did Dakari Johnson lead the Wildcats in rebounds?
   a) 7
   b) 8
   c) 9
   d) 10

Q352: Who led the 2014-15 Wildcats in scoring with 11 points per game?
   a) Devin Booker
   b) Aaron Harrison
   c) Karl-Anthony Towns
   d) Andrew Harrison

Q353: True or False: No 2014-15 Wildcats averaged 26 or more minutes of playing time per game.

Q354: What 2014-15 Wildcat had the highest three-point field goal percentage with 42.9%?
   a) Devin Booker

b) Aaron Harrison
c) Tyler Ulis
d) Andrew Harrison

Q355: Name the recruit who committed to U.K. in June 2015 after reclassifying from the Class of 2016. He joined 2015 "Next Cats" Isaiah Briscoe, Skal Labissiere, Isaac Humphries and Mychal Mulder.

Q356: In November 2015, U.K. climbed to a number one ranking for the fifth year in Calipari's seven years at Kentucky. An 87-77 loss to UCLA dropped U.K.'s all-time record when ranked number one to 218-28 (.886). True or False: This winning percentage is the highest of all-time for schools with the top ranking.

Q357: The loss against UCLA also snapped U.K.'s regular season winning streak. How many regular season games did the Wildcats win before their loss to the Bruins?
a) 38
b) 39
c) 40
d) 41

Q358: What 2015-16 Wildcat scored 21 points and grabbed 13 rebounds against Eastern Kentucky University?
a) Alex Poythress
b) Jamal Murray
c) Marcus Lee
d) Skal Labissiere

Q359: Who scored 33 points in U.K.'s 74-67 loss to Ohio State?
a) Alex Poythress
b) Jamal Murray
c) Isaiah Briscoe
d) Skal Labissiere

Q360: Who was named SEC Freshman of the Week after he scored 18 points against Illinois State and 20 points against UCLA?
a) Isaac Humphries
b) Jamal Murray
c) Isaiah Briscoe
d) Skal Labissiere

ANSWERS 346-360

A346: The only other teams in NCAA history to win 38 games in a season were the 2007-08 Memphis Tigers and the 2011-12 national champion Kentucky Wildcats. All three teams were coached by Calipari!

A347: True.

A348: UCLA's John Wooden and Duke's Mike Krzyzewski.

A349: 2012 Kentucky national champion Kyle Wiltjer was also named a Top Ten John Wooden All-American finalist for his incredible season with Gonzaga.

A350: D. 25.

A351: C. Nine.

A352: B. Aaron Harrison.

A353: True.

A354: C. Tyler Ulis.

A355: Jamal Murray.

A356: True.

A357: A. 38.

A358: A. Alex Poythress.

A359: B. Jamal Murray. Murray would later score 35 points to lead U.K. to victory in a 80-61 thrashing of SEC rival Florida. He is the first freshman in U.K. history with two 30-point games.

A360: C. Isaiah Briscoe.

QUESTIONS 361-375

Q361: On December 26, 2015, Kentucky beat in-state rival Louisville 75-73 at Rupp Arena. The Wildcats improved their series record to 34-15 over the Cardinals. Kentucky is 15-2 when both teams are ranked. What is Kentucky's record against Louisville when Coach Calipari has been at the helm?

    a) 9-0
    b) 8-1
    c) 7-2
    d) 6-3

Q362: Fresh off his SEC Player of the Week honors, Tyler Ulis scored 21 points and dished out eight assists against Louisville. A season earlier, Ulis had scored 14 points against the Cardinals. He shot a combined 6 of 9 from three-point range vs. Louisville. How many turnovers did Ulis commit in his 65 minutes of total play against Louisville?

    a) 3
    b) 2
    c) 1
    d) 0

Q363: How many total three-pointers did the Wildcats sink in their 75-73 win over Louisville?

    a) 13
    b) 12
    c) 11
    d) 10

Q364: Name the Kentucky native who scored 13 points off the bench to help propel the Wildcats over the Cardinals. HINT: His last two free throws were the Wildcats final points in their 75-73 win.

Q365: Who was the last Kentucky native to score in double-digits against the Cardinals? Hint: He scored in double-digits against Louisville in the 2012 Final Four.

Q366: On January 2, 2016, Kentucky snapped Mississippi's seven-game winning streak with an easy 83-61 win at Rupp Arena in its first SEC game of the season. This was Kentucky's 2,189th win of all-time. True or False: Kentucky is the winningest school in NCAA history.

Q367: Tyler Ulis scored 20 points and dished out ten assists in Kentucky's win over Ole Miss. Name the last Wildcat who had ten assists in one game.

a) Julius Mays
b) Marquis Teague
c) Saul Smith
d) John Wall

Q368: Jamal Murray made a three-pointer in each of Kentucky's first 27 games of the 2015-16 season. True or False: Murray was the first Wildcat to hit a three-pointer in 27 consecutive games to start a season.

Q369: Tyler Ulis' 20 point effort against Mississippi gave him back-to-back 20-point games. Who was the last Wildcat to accomplish this feat?
a) James Young
b) Julius Randle
c) Aaron Harrison
d) Karl-Anthony Towns

Q370: Name the Wildcat who made 6 of 9 field goals against Mississippi. HINT: He was in the midst of a seven-game stretch that saw him make 32 of 43 shots for a staggering 74.4% field goal percentage.
a) Skal Labissiere
b) Marcus Lee
c) Derek Willis
d) Alex Poythress

Q371: Coach Calipari's 200th Kentucky win came against rival Louisville. True or False: He became the fastest coach (fewest number of games) in Division 1 history to win 200 games for a school.

Q372: True or False: Coach Calipari is the only Division 1 coach to ever win 189 games with three different teams.

Q373: After Kentucky's win over Mississippi State on January 12, 2016, Coach Calipari's record at Rupp Arena was an incredible 112-4. How many of those four losses came from non-conference opponents?

Q374: The future continues to look bright for Big Blue Nation during the Calipari Era. Four "Next Cats" from the Class of 2016 were selected to compete during the 2016 McDonald's All-American Game in March. Name these four "Next Cats" McDonald's All-Americans.

Q375: This 6' 11" "Next Cat"—a five-star power forward from Lynchburg, Virginia—will be joining the 2016-17 Wildcats.

ANSWERS 361-375

A361: B. 8-1.

A362: C. One.

A363: C. 11.

A364: Dominique Hawkins.

A365: Darius Miller.

A366: True. U.K.'s 2,189 wins as of January 2, 2016, make them the winningest school of all-time!

A367: A. Julius Mays was the last Wildcat to dish out double-digit assists in Kentucky's win over Lafayette on November 16, 2012.

A368: True. *At the time this book was printed Jamal Murray's three-pointer streak was still active.

A369: A. James Young.

A370: B. Marcus Lee.

A371: False. Clair Bee was 200-31 when he coached LIU-Brooklyn from 1931-41. Calipari was the second fastest coach to reach 200 wins for a school; his record was 200-40 when he beat Louisville to record his 200th win.

A372: True.

A373: Only one of Calipari's four losses at Rupp Arena came from a non-conference opponent.

A374: Edrice Adebayo from Jacksonville, NC; Wenyen Gabriel from Wilbraham, MA; De'Aaron Fox from Katy, TX; Malik Monk from Bentonville, AR.

A375: Sacha Killeya-Jones.

"He who controlleth the backboard, controlleth the game."
— Adolph Rupp

6 THE RECORDS

It's been said that records are made to be broken. Well, I would argue some Kentucky records are likely never to be broken. Kentucky career records are likely to remain unbroken for quite some time because most of Kentucky's top players are "one and done" or are destined to "succeed and then proceed" as Kentucky fans and Calipari have begun describing players who enter the NBA draft early. However, some records like Kentucky losing to a team by 70 points are certainly never going to be broken! And as long as Calipari keeps bringing in top recruiting class after top recruiting class, there is just no way another player could average 33.9 points per game like Dan Issel did during the 1969-70 season. And how about the national record Kentucky set for most rebounds in a game against Ole Miss on February 8, 1964? 108! "Are you serious? 108?" I write with the most intense Dick Vitale voice possible! I would argue records are made to mark time and recall them saying, "Remember when ..."

QUESTIONS 376-390

Q376: How many Wildcats are in the 1,000 point club?
a) 55
b) 57
c) 60
d) 62

Q377: Name the three Wildcats who are in the 2,000 point club.

Q378: Who holds Kentucky's record for highest career scoring average?

Q379: Who holds the record for most games played in a career?
a) Keith Bogans
b) Ralph Beard
c) Jamaal Magloire
d) Darius Miller

Q380: What Wildcat team set a school record when it scored 3,325 points in a season?
a) 1995-96
b) 1996-97
c) 2011-12
d) 2014-15

Q381: The 1970-71 team hit the century mark in points more than any other team in school history. How many times did these Wildcats score 100 or more points?
a) 15
b) 17
c) 10
d) 12

Q382: Kenny Walker made 11 of 11 field goal attempts in a game against Western Kentucky University on March 16, 1986. Name the Wildcat who sank 12 of 12 field goal attempts in a game against Morehead on December 17, 1993.
a) Travis Ford
b) Rodney Dent
c) Jared Prickett
d) Tony Delk

Q383: True or False: Kentucky once scored 113 points in a game … and *lost*.

Q384: What was Dan Issel's career scoring average?
a) 25.8
b) 26.4
c) 26.9
d) 27.3

Q385: Kentucky set a record for most three-pointers made in one game against North Carolina on December 27, 1989. How many three-pointers did the Wildcats make that day against the Tar Heels?
a) 16
b) 17
c) 19
d) 21

Q386: How many career three-pointers did Tony Delk sink as a Wildcat from 1993-96 to set the school record?
a) 264
b) 271
c) 283
d) 294

Q387: Doron Lamb holds the school record for highest career three-point field goal percentage. What was Lamb's shooting percentage from beyond the arc?
a) 45%
b) 46.5%
c) 47%
d) 47.5%

Q388: The 2011-12 national champion Wildcats hold the school record for most blocks in a season. How many shots did U.K. block during this memorable season?
a) 316
b) 327
c) 344
d) 351

Q389: Kentucky's worst ever defeat was 87-17. Who beat the Wildcats so badly?

Q390: Kentucky holds the national record for most consecutive home wins. During what years did the Wildcats win 129 consecutive home games?

ANSWERS 376-390

A376: C. 60.

A377: Dan Issel (2,138), Kenny Walker (2,080) and Jack Givens (2,038).

A378: Dan Issel averaged 25.8 points throughout his Kentucky career.

A379: D. Darius Miller played in a record 152 games for Kentucky!

A380: B. 1996-97.

A381: A. 15.

A382: B. Rodney Dent.

A383: True. Kentucky lost to Southwest Louisiana 116-113 on December 23, 1990.

A384: A. 258.

A385: D. 21.

A386: C. 283.

A387: D. 47.5%. Doron Lamb made 144 of 303 career three-point attempts.

A388: C. 344.

A389: Centre College beat Kentucky 87-17 on January 28, 1910.

A390: 1943-55.

QUESTIONS 391-405

Q391: What Wildcat made 104 of 114 free throw attempts in 1979-80 to set the school record (with minimum of 50 attempts) for free throw percentage at 91.2%?

Q392: Bob Burrow (1955) and Bill Spivey (1951) share the school record for most rebounds in a game. How many rebounds did they both secure in one game to set the school record?
   a) 26
   b) 29
   c) 32
   d) 34

Q393: What Wildcat holds the school record for most assists in one game?

Q394: Wayne Turner and Rajon Rondo share a Kentucky record. What record is it?

Q395: What amazing feat was Travis Ford the first Wildcat to ever accomplish?

Q396: Who made 16 consecutive free throws in a game against Ole Miss on January 2, 1952?

Q397: Kentucky set a school record for most points scored in one game when they beat the Georgia Bulldogs in Louisville's Armory on February 27, 1956. How many points did the Wildcats score in this epic blowout?
   a) 136
   b) 139
   c) 143
   d) 146

Q398: On January 16, 1996, U.K. set a school record for most points scored in the first half of a game. How many first half points did the Wildcats score that day against the LSU Tigers?
   a) 83
   b) 86
   c) 89
   d) 93

Q399: The 1996-97 Wildcats hold the Kentucky record for most steals in a season. How many steals did they collect in their 40 games?
   a) 480
   b) 491

c) 502

d) 510

Q400: In a game against Notre Dame on December 29, 1981, Kentucky set a record for the highest team field goal percentage in a game. What did the Wildcats shoot from the floor that night?

a) 72.5%

b) 75%

c) 76.5%

d) 78%

Q401: Dan Issel set the school record for points during the 1969-70 season. How many points did he score?

a) 798

b) 837

c) 921

d) 948

Q402: How many three-pointers did Jodie Meeks sink in 36 games during the 2008-09 season?

a) 108

b) 117

c) 123

d) 128

Q403: What Kentucky record do Ramel Bradley, Keith Bogans, Tayshaun Prince and Jamal Mashburn share?

Q404: How many consecutive games did the Wildcats win at Rupp Arena from November 11, 2009, through March 1, 2012?

a) 50

b) 51

c) 52

d) 53

Q405: Dwight Anderson set a school record for most free throws made in a game. How many free throws did he make against Mississippi State on January 15, 1979?

a) 16

b) 17

c) 18

d) 19

ANSWERS 391-405

A391: Kyle Macy. Macy also shares the school record for highest career free throw percentage with Jodie Meeks. Both Macy and Meeks shot 89% from the free throw line while playing for Kentucky.

A392: D. 34.

A393: John Wall dished out a school record 16 assists in a game against Hartford on December 29, 2009. Wall also holds the Kentucky record for most assists in a season with 241.

A394: Wayne Turner and Rajon Rondo share the school record for most steals in one game. Both Turner and Rondo swiped eight steals in one game!

A395: Travis Ford made 50 consecutive free throws in a 14-game stretch during the 1992-93 and 1993-94 seasons.

A396: Cliff Hagan.

A397: C. 143.

A398: B. 86.

A399: A. 480.

A400: C. 76.5%.

A401: D. 948.

A402: B. 117.

A403: Ramel Bradley, Keith Bogans, Tayshaun Prince and Jamal Mashburn all made 5 of 5 three-point attempts in a game to share the highest three-point field goal percentage in a game (five attempts minimum).

A404: B. 51.

A405: C. 18.

QUESTIONS 406-410

Q406: True or False: Dan Issel is the Kentucky career leader in both points and rebounds.

Q407: Jamaal Magloire is the all-time leading Wildcat shot blocker. Who had the second most blocked shots for Kentucky?
a) Willie Cauley-Stein
b) Melvin Turpin
c) Sam Bowie
d) Andre Riddick

Q408: What Wildcat holds the school record for most points scored in a season by a freshman?
a) Brandon Knight
b) Julius Randle
c) Archie Goodwin
d) John Wall

Q409: Who is the all-time leading scorer for Kentucky guards?
a) Ed Davender
b) Tony Delk
c) Keith Bogans
d) Mike Casey

Q410: Who are the only Wildcats to be named to the All-NCAA Final Four team twice? HINT: Both achieved this honor in back-to-back years and one earned the NCAA Tournament Most Outstanding Player award both years.

ANSWERS 406-410

A406: True. Dan Issel holds the Kentucky record for most points in a career and he also holds the school record for most rebounds in a career with 1,078!

A407: A. Willie Cauley-Stein.

A408: A. Brandon Knight. Knight scored 657 points in 2011.

A409: C. Keith Bogans. Bogans scored 1,923 career points.

A410: Alex Groza (1948 and 1949) and Scott Padgett (1997 and 1998). Groza was also named NCAA Tournament Most Outstanding Player in 1948 and 1949.

"The best teams I've had, had a little bit of a swagger."
— John Calipari

7 THE COACHES

Coach John Calipari recorded his 200th win with Kentucky during the 2015-16 season. Calipari became the fifth Kentucky coach to collect 200 wins. Adolph Rupp, Joe B. Hall, Rick Pitino, Tubby Smith and John Calipari are the five legends who have made Kentucky arguably the all-time best basketball school in the country.

QUESTIONS 411-425

Q411: True or False: Kentucky is the only Division 1 school in the country to have had five coaches win over 200 games.

Q412: Name the Kentucky coach who is recognized for his willingness to recruit black players to help the school overcome its "white players only" image.

Q413: Legendary coach Adolph Rupp built a dynasty. His coaching record was an amazing 876-190 for an 82.2 winning percentage. How many years did he coach?
- a) 40
- b) 41
- c) 42
- d) 43

Q414: Where did Coach Rupp attend college and play basketball?
- a) Kansas
- b) Iowa
- c) Oklahoma
- d) Missouri

Q415: Coach Phog Allen mentored Adolph Rupp. Allen studied under Dr. James Naismith who invented basketball. What year did Naismith invent this beloved national pastime?

Q416: Why was Rupp's 747th career win—against Dayton on March 12, 1966—so significant?

Q417: Coach Rupp became the all-time winningest college basketball coach on February 18, 1967, when the Wildcats beat Mississippi State on the road. Who did Rupp pass on the all-time wins list?

Q418: Name the coach who passed Rupp on the all-time wins list in 1997.

Q419: Coach Rupp was named the national Coach of the Year four times. How many times did he win SEC Coach of the Year?
- a) 7
- b) 9
- c) 12
- d) 15

Q420: Coach Rupp was known as the "The ... of the Bluegrass" and "The Man in the ... Suit." Complete both quotes.

Q421: How many SEC titles did Rupp's teams win?
 a) 15
 b) 21
 c) 25
 d) 27

Q422: What year did Rupp coach a gold medalist Olympic basketball team?

Q423: Rupp's teams won four NCAA championships. How many times were his teams ranked number one in a season's final polls?
 a) 4
 b) 6
 c) 8
 d) 9

Q424: How many of Rupp's players were named All-Americans?
 a) 20
 b) 21
 c) 22
 d) 23

Q425: What honor did Rupp receive in 1969?

ANSWERS 411-425

A411: True. Kentucky is the only Division 1 school to boast five coaches with 200-plus wins. Division 1 schools with four 200-win coaches: Alabama, Kansas, Maryland and Villanova.

A412: Joe B. Hall.

A413: C. 42. Rupp coached at Kentucky from 1930-72.

A414: A. Kansas.

A415: 1891.

A416: Rupp's 747th win passed his mentor Phog Allen on the all-time winningest coaches list.

A417: Ed Diddle from Western Kentucky.

A418: Dean Smith from North Carolina.

A419: A. Seven.

A420: "The *Baron* of the Bluegrass" and "The Man in the *Brown* Suit."

A421: D. 27.

A422: 1948.

A423: B. Six.

A424: D. 23.

A425: Rupp was elected into the Naismith Memorial Basketball Hall of Fame.

QUESTIONS 426-440

Q426: Adolph Rupp retired in 1972, and Joe B. Hall was tasked to fill his shoes. However, as a native of Cynthiana, Kentucky, former Wildcat basketball player and assistant coach, Hall proved he had the mettle to be a successful Kentucky coach. How many years did he serve as Kentucky's head coach?
  a) 10
  b) 11
  c) 13
  d) 15

Q427: True or False: Coach Hall won over 300 games as the head coach of Kentucky.

Q428: How many of Coach Hall's teams made it to the Final Four?
  a) 2
  b) 3
  c) 4
  d) 5

Q429: In what year did Coach Hall and the Wildcats win the NIT?
  a) 1975
  b) 1976
  c) 1978
  d) 1979

Q430: In what year did Coach Hall and the Wildcats win the NCAA national championship?
  a) 1975
  b) 1976
  c) 1978
  d) 1979

Q431: Name the team Coach Hall was part of as it traveled throughout Europe in 1951.

Q432: True or False: Coach Hall played basketball for Kentucky during "The Fabulous Five" era.

Q433: Name the Kentucky high school where Coach Hall started his coaching career.

Q434: How many of Coach Hall's Wildcats were drafted by the NBA?
  a) 19

b) 23
c) 25
d) 29

Q435: How many SEC titles did Coach Hall's teams win?
a) 8
b) 9
c) 10
d) 11

Q436: Eddie Sutton took over the head coaching position at Kentucky in 1985. Where did Sutton coach prior to becoming a Wildcat?
a) Alabama
b) Arkansas
c) Missouri
d) Tennessee

Q437: What were Coach Sutton's teams best known for?
a) Fastbreaks
b) Defense
c) Rebounding
d) Scoring

Q438: What was the record of Coach Sutton's first Kentucky team (1985-86) that earned the school an Elite Eight NCAA Tournament appearance and earned Sutton national Coach of the Year honors?
a) 29-7
b) 30-6
c) 31-5
d) 32-4

Q439: Coach Sutton's third Kentucky team started the 1987-88 season with an impressive undefeated streak that included wins over Louisville and Indiana to earn a number one ranking. How long was its streak at the start of the season?
a) 10-0
b) 11-0
c) 12-0
d) 13-0

Q440: Coach Sutton's final Kentucky team finished the 1988-89 season with the school's first losing record since 1927! What was the team's final record?
a) 12-20
b) 13-19
c) 14-18

d) 15-17

ANSWERS 426-440

A426: C. 13.

A427: False. Coach Hall's record was an impressive 297-100 for a winning percentage of 74.8.

A428: B. Three.

A429: B. 1976.

A430: C. 1978.

A431: Harlem Globetrotters.

A432: True. Coach Hall admitted that although he played during "The Fabulous Five" era, he was one of the "Sorry Seven".

A433: Shepherdsville High School (1956).

A434: B. 23.

A435: A. Eight.

A436: B. Arkansas.

A437: B. Defense.

A438: D. 32-4.

A439: A. 10-0.

A440: B. 13-19.

QUESTIONS 441-455

Q441: Rick Pitino took over as Kentucky's next head coach in 1989 and engineered a quick and remarkable turnaround for the program. How old was Pitino when he accepted the U.K. position?
  a) 35
  b) 36
  c) 37
  d) 38

Q442: Name the last three teams Pitino coached before taking over for the Wildcats.

Q443: In 1990, Rick Pitino hired the first female assistant men's basketball coach in Division 1 history. She later became the U.K. Lady Wildcats head coach and led the Lady Wildcats to their first ever 20-win season and their first NCAA Tournament win in 17 years. Name this coach.

Q444: Pitino's keys to success were the three-point shot and a full-court press. Why did he call his teams' press "The Mother-in-law Press"?

Q445: Pitino's first team stunned basketball fans when the Wildcats beat a number nine-ranked LSU team that featured Shaquille O'Neal and Chris Jackson. The final score was 100-95. What was the nickname of Pitino's first team?

Q446: What was U.K.'s 1991 SEC record?
  a) 12-6
  b) 13-5
  c) 14-4
  d) 15-3

Q447: In 1992, Pitino coached Kentucky in what many people have called the greatest college basketball game ever played. Sadly, "Pitino's Unforgettables" lost in heart-breaking fashion after Duke's Christian Laettner sank a last-second game-winning shot. What was the final score of this historic game?

Q448: How far did Pitino's 1994-95 Wildcats advance in the NCAA Tournament?

Q449: Although four of Pitino's 1996 national champions were drafted and Derek Anderson's 1996-97 season ended early with an injury, the Wildcats still completed a remarkable season. How far did Kentucky advance in the 1997 NCAA Tournament?

Q450: Pitino won 5 of 6 SEC Tournament titles while coaching for Kentucky. What was his SEC Tournament record?

Q451: The NBA drafted eight of Pitino's Wildcats. How many were lottery picks?
- a) 2
- b) 3
- c) 4
- d) 5

Q452: Rick Pitino left UK for the NBA in 1997. What team did he coach?

Q453: In his first season with Kentucky, coach Tubby Smith led the Wildcats to an SEC title, SEC Tournament title and NCAA national championship. With this historic season, Smith set a NCAA coaching record for the most wins by a coach during his first year at a school. How many wins did the Wildcats have during this 1997-98 season?
- a) 32
- b) 33
- c) 34
- d) 35

Q454: The Wildcats trailed Utah at halftime in the national championship game. How many points were they behind at the break?
- a) 7
- b) 8
- c) 10
- d) 12

Q455: True or False: Tubby Smith was named both the 1998 SEC Coach of the Year and national Coach of the Year.

ANSWERS 441-455

A441: B. 36.

A442: New York Knicks, Providence, Boston College. Pitino guided all three of these programs to quick turnarounds, just like he did with Kentucky.

A443: Bernadette Locke-Mattox. She was also the first Georgia Lady Bulldog to earn both All-American and Academic All-American honors—and she led the Bulldogs to an NIT championship in 1981.

A444: Pitino called it "The Mother-in-law Press" because of its "constant harassment and pressure."

A445: "Pitino's Bombino's".

A446: C. 14-4.

A447: 104-103.

A448: Elite Eight.

A449: The 1996-97 Wildcats advanced to the national championship game but lost to Arizona 84-79.

A450: 17-1.

A451: B. Three.

A452: Boston Celtics.

A453: D. 35 wins.

A454: C. Ten.

A455: True.

QUESTIONS 456-470

Q456: What was the style of play called that the Wildcats performed while under Tubby Smith?

Q457: Tubby Smith's second team finished 28-9, won the SEC Tournament, and reached the Elite Eight. Name the team that stopped them from advancing to the Final Four.
a) Michigan State
b) Michigan
c) Duke
d) Indiana

Q458: Tubby Smith's 2002-03 team boasted another impressive record. What was Kentucky's record that year?
a) 29-5
b) 32-4
c) 30-6
d) 33-5

Q459: True or False: At the time, Tubby Smith recorded 100 Kentucky wins faster than any other U.K. coach in school history.

Q460: What was Tubby Smith's winning percentage during his ten years as Kentucky's coach?
a) 74%
b) 76%
c) 78%
d) 80%

Q461: Where did Tubby Smith coach after leaving Kentucky?

Q462: How many siblings does Tubby Smith have?

Q463: Name the 2000 U.S. Olympic basketball head coach who asked Tubby Smith to be one of his assistant coaches.

Q464: Billy Gillispie took over as the Wildcats next head coach. Name the two college programs Gillispie successfully coached prior to Kentucky.

Q465: Gillispie's first Kentucky team started the season 6-7. What was its record in the SEC that year?
a) 12-4
b) 11-5
c) 10-6

d) 9-7

Q466: Name the school that beat Gillispie's first Kentucky team in the first round of the NCAA Tournament.
   a) DePaul
   b) Syracuse
   c) Marquette
   d) Memphis

Q467: Gillispie's second team finished 22-14 but failed to make it to the NCAA Tournament. When was the last time U.K. failed to make the field for the NCAA Tournament?
   a) 1989
   b) 1991
   c) 1994
   d) 2000

Q468: John Calipari took over as head coach of the Wildcats in 2009. During his first season in Big Blue Nation, Calipari led Kentucky to a 35-3 record. How many consecutive seasons did Coach Calipari's Memphis teams win 30 or more games?
   a) 2
   b) 3
   c) 4
   d) 5

Q469: True or False: Coach Calipari's second Kentucky team lost in the Elite Eight.

Q470: Coach Calipari led the Memphis Tigers for nine successful seasons before coming to Kentucky. What was his winning percentage at Memphis?
   a) 76%
   b) 77.5%
   c) 78.5%
   d) 80%

ANSWERS 456-470

A456: "Tubby Ball".

A457: A. Michigan State.

A458: B. 32-4.

A459: False. At the time, Tubby Smith was the second fastest Kentucky coach to record 100 wins.

A460: B. 76%.

A461: Tulsa. Tubby Smith helped Tulsa earn two Sweet Sixteen appearances and finished with a 79-43 record while at the school.

A462: 16.

A463: Larry Brown.

A464: Texas A&M and University of Texas El Paso (UTEP).

A465: A. 12-4. Gillispie won the SEC co-Coach of the Year award.

A466: C. Marquette.

A467: B. 1991.

A468: C. Four.

A469: False. Kentucky's 2010-11 team advanced to the Final Four.

A470: C. 78.5%.

QUESTIONS 471-475

Q471: Before coaching at Memphis, Calipari coached at Massachusetts from 1988 through 1996. What was his winning percentage at UMass?
   a) 70%
   b) 71.5%
   c) 73%
   d) 75%

Q472: What was the record of Coach Calipari's 1995-96 UMass team?
   a) 32-5
   b) 33-4
   c) 34-3
   d) 35-2

Q473: In spring 2015, Coach Calipari became the 96th coach to be elected to the Naismith Memorial Basketball Hall of Fame in Springfield, Massachusetts. Calipari was also named the 2015 Naismith College Coach of the Year for the third time in his career. What is significant about Calipari's three Coach of the Year honors?

Q474: True or False: Coach Calipari is the only coach who has had three players selected as the top pick in the NBA draft.

Q475: Who coached the Wildcats to a perfect 9-0 season in 1912?
   a) J.J. Tigert
   b) E.R. Sweetland
   c) John Mauer
   d) Ray Eklund

ANSWERS 471-475

A471: C. 73%.

A472: D. 35-2.

A473: Calipari became the first coach to win the Naismith College Coach of the Year award for three different schools. Calipari won with Massachusetts in 1996, Memphis in 2008, and Kentucky in 2015.

A474: True.

A475: B. E.R. Sweetland.

"Enough talking. Let's ball."
— John Calipari

8 50-50 BALLS

This last chapter is a smorgasbord of questions. Let's call these miscellaneous questions "loose balls," or as Coach Calipari calls them, "50-50 balls." How many times have we heard Calipari stress the importance of coming out on top of these 50-50 balls? What does it take to win a 50-50 ball? It takes fierce focus, determination, tenacity, heart, 100% effort, and a little crazy! And that is exactly what you will need if you are going to come out on top of these questions. Calipari works all year to create fighters out of his talented players because he knows that is ultimately the surest way to the number one spot. Now you too must dig deep! Finish strong and see where you rank among the thousands of ultimate Wildcats fans in Big Blue Nation. You might just be Kentucky's ultimate fan.

QUESTIONS 476-490

Q476: What 1980s fashion trend did Kentucky fan-favorite Josh Harrellson wear during his recruiting visit? HINT: This article of clothing quickly became Harrellson's nickname.

Q477: S.A. Boles coached the 1918 Kentucky team to a 9-2-1 record. Why did one of the games end in a tie?

Q478: True or False: Coach Rupp retired mid-season because he was experiencing health issues.

Q479: What team blew Kentucky away 107-83 in the 1970-71 Mideast Regional in Athens, Georgia?

Q480: The most points any player has ever scored against a Kentucky team is 66. Who accomplished this feat in 1970?

Q481: True or False: Not one Kentucky starter scored a field goal in the second half of the 1984 Final Four game against Patrick Ewing and Georgetown.

Q482: What 1996 national champion Wildcat presented President Clinton with a U.K. jersey?

Q483: What business did Joe B. Hall enter after his coaching career?

Q484: What Wildcat hit a clutch 13-foot jump shot over Christian Laettner to give Kentucky a 103-102 lead over Duke with 2.1 seconds left in the 1992 Elite Eight epic battle?

Q485: Who recorded U.K.'s first ever triple-double with 19 points, ten rebounds, and ten assists in a game against Austin Peay?

Q486: Rex Chapman's freshman year was the first year of the three-pointer. What was Chapman's three-point field goal percentage his sophomore year that helped him become the first Kentucky sophomore to join the 1,000 point club?
   a) 38.5%
   b) 40%
   c) 41.5%
   d) 42.5%

Q487: Whose father was the "Emery Package" containing $1,000 intended for?

Q488: What was the total home, road and neutral courts attendance for

"The Unbeatables" during the 2014-15 season?
    a) 844,435
    b) 937,392
    c) 1,076,365
    d) 1,143,779

Q489: True or False: At the start of the 2015-16 season, Kentucky's all-time winning percentage at Rupp Arena was over 90%.

Q490: True or False: Kentucky has never lost three consecutive games at Rupp Arena.

ANSWERS 476-490

A476: Josh Harrellson wore jean shorts, also known as "jorts," to his Kentucky recruiting visit. Soon thereafter Harrellson's nickname became "Jorts." Follow Harrellson's Twitter account @BigJorts55 to see him playing professional basketball overseas.

A477: A scorer's mistake discovered after the game resulted in a tie.

A478: False. Coach Rupp retired when he turned 70 because that was the mandatory retirement age for all University of Kentucky employees. Despite many petitions and other efforts, no exception was made for Rupp.

A479: The Western Kentucky University Hilltoppers beat the Wildcats 107-83 in the Mideast Regional. WKU's team featured many black players who were Kentucky prep stars.

A480: LSU's "Pistol" Pete Maravich scored 66 points in one game against the Wildcats.

A481: True. Not one Wildcat starter scored a field goal in the second half of the 1984 Final Four game against Georgetown. In fact, the Wildcats shot 3 of 33 from the field in the second half. The team's 40 points were the lowest total in any Final Four game since the 1949 Wildcats beat Oklahoma 46-36 in the championship game.

A482: Mark Pope.

A483: Joe B. Hall entered the world of banking after his coaching career ended.

A484: Sean Woods.

A485: Chris Mills.

A486: C. 41.5%.

A487: Chris Mills.

A488: A. 844,435. Rupp Arena hosted 447,874 fans—another 145,211 spectators watched the team at away games and 251,350 fans watched the team on neutral courts.

A489: False. At the start of the 2015-16 season, Kentucky's record at Rupp Arena was 528-64, an 89.2 winning percentage.

A490: True.

QUESTIONS 491-505

Q491: Name the Kentucky player whose "Three-pointer Heard Around the World" almost did not happen because he flunked too many classes his freshman year and lost his eligibility.

Q492: What All-American Kentucky player was banned from playing Kentucky sports?

Q493: What season did the NCAA suspend Kentucky's basketball program?

Q494: Name the celebrity Kentucky basketball fan who said, "One thing I love about going to U.K. games is that I don't feel like a movie star; I'm just another passionate fan."

Q495: What all-state high school center from Lawrenceburg, Kentucky, earned three national championship rings with the Kentucky Wildcats?

Q496: Name the Kentucky legend whose play-by-play radio for both Kentucky basketball and the Cincinnati Reds was cut short when he passed away at 42.

Q497: Name the Kentucky legend who won an NBA championship with the Detroit Pistons in 2004 and an Olympic gold medal in Beijing in 2008.

Q498: What Kentucky walk-on finished with an impressive 730 career points and 364 career assists?

Q499: In January 2016, the U.K. cheerleading squad won another national championship! How many national titles has Kentucky won since its first championship in 1985?
- a) 12
- b) 15
- c) 18
- d) 20

Q500: What 1988 McDonald's High School All-American from Indiana verbally committed to Kentucky but never played a game for the Wildcats? HINT: Shortly after high school, he went on to play in the NBA for 14 seasons.

Q501: Where did the 2008-09 Wildcats play their first round NIT game against UNLV? HINT: This was the first time the Wildcats played there since 1976.

Q502: True or False: Every Wildcat but one scored in a 106-44 rout over Vanderbilt during the 2002-03 season.

Q503: The 2003-04 Wildcats played 32 games. In how many of those games did they hold a double-digit lead?
    a) 27
    b) 29
    c) 30
    d) 32

Q504: On January 16, 2016, Tyler Ulis scored 17 points, grabbed ten rebounds and dished out eight assists. He was just two assists shy of becoming only the second player in U.K. history to record a triple-double. How tall is Ulis?

Q505: What Kentucky recruit did coaches Joe B. Hall, John Calipari, Rick Pitino, Bruce Pearl and author of this book, Joel Katte, watch at the Joe B. Hall Bluegrass Classic at Paul Laurence Dunbar High School in Lexington, Kentucky on November 28, 2014?

ANSWERS 491-505

A491: Scott Padgett. Padgett regrouped in the classroom, earning his eligibility back nearly a year-and-a-half later. He became a very successful player and student. Padgett earned Academic All-SEC honors twice!

A492: Bill Spivey.

A493: 1952-53.

A494: Ashley Judd.

A495: Equipment Manager Bill "Mr. Wildcat" Keightley earned three national championship rings during his 48 years of work with the team. The former high school standout was affectionately known as "Mr. Bill".

A496: Claude Sullivan. Sullivan was elected to the Kentucky Journalism Hall of Fame and the U.K. Sports Hall of Fame for his service and professionalism.

A497: Tayshaun Prince.

A498: Saul Smith. Smith was Tubby Smith's middle son.

A499: D. 20. The Kentucky cheerleading team has won an incredible 21 national titles! U.K. cheerleaders won eight national championships in a row from 1995 through 2002!

A500: Shawn Kemp.

A501: 8,000+ fans packed into Memorial Coliseum to watch the Wildcats play their 2009 NIT game against UNLV.

A502: False. Every Wildcat scored!

A503: A. 27.

A504: 5' 9". Remarkably, Ulis grabbed ten rebounds against Auburn and missed a triple-double by only two assists!

A505: Jamal Murray.

BONUS: KENTUCKY DERBY IQ

INTRODUCTION

SPYING THE TWIN SPIRES, hugging the rail, hearing the snap of the gate, the crowd takes a nervous deep breath in unison. The horses lunge, the jockeys crouch. Now the race for the roses is run and timelessness has begun.

Long-shot odds, winning tickets, record crowds, Hall of Fame statistics, and historical dates all add up to the "Most exciting two minutes in sports." Think you know Kentucky Derby history?

Think again.

This IQ Series book will test even the best horsemen and trainers who have been around the sport their whole lives.

Test your skills. Wrack your brain. It's the ultimate Kentucky Derby IQ test.

You might be slow out of the gate. Maybe you will lunge to an early lead but fade to finish last. Perhaps you will pace yourself but eventually realize you don't have the pedigree to compete in a Triple Crown race. Regardless of your performance, go back and reread each chapter, and memorize every fun, fascinating Derby fact. When you can answer 90% or more of the 260 questions, you have achieved ultimate fan status!

1 MORNING WORKOUTS

"If you can figure out a way to visit the backstretch of Churchill Downs for morning workouts during Derby week, any begging you had to do will be worth it. With trainers and clockers leaning on the rail, workout riders hurrying to grab their next mounts, grooms hosing off steaming horses, the sound of hoofbeats, and galloping horses emerging from the morning fog, this is heaven for the true aficionado ... You are actually close enough to see the horses' breath and hear the rhythms of their exertion."
— Sheri Seggerman and Mary Tiegreen, *The Kentucky Derby: 101 Reasons to Love America's Favorite Horse Race*

EVERY GOOD RIDE STARTS with a good warm up. Walking, listening to the horse, and avoiding anything that feels like work are essential for an effective warm up.

The same holds true for this book.

Go at a pace that works for you. Push yourself but remember to pull back just enough to save whatever energy and adrenaline is needed for your glorious win-by-a-nose photo finish.

However, if you start cramping in warm-ups, it will likely be a grueling, humbling ride ...

Question 1: The Kentucky Derby is always held on which day?
　　a) The first Sunday in March
　　b) The first Sunday in April
　　c) The first Saturday in May
　　d) The first Sunday in May

Question 2: The first race was run in what year?
　　a) 1870
　　b) 1872
　　c) 1875
　　d) 1876

Question 3: True or False: The Kentucky Derby is the last of the Triple Crown races.

Question 4: Considered by many racing experts to be the greatest Thoroughbred of all time, this horse was born on March 29, 1917 in Lexington, Kentucky. He won 20 of his 21 career starts, including eight races in record time.

a) Sir Barton
b) Lexington
c) Regret
d) Man o' War

Question 5: True or False: Kentucky Statesman Cassius Clay was one of the men who helped form the Commonwealth's first Jockey Club.

ANSWER KEY

1. C. The Kentucky Derby runs the first Saturday of May.

2. C. The first Derby was in 1875.

3. False. The Kentucky Derby is the first of the Triple Crown races.

4. D. Man o' War.

5. False. Not Cassius Clay! Rather, Kentucky Statesman Henry Clay helped establish the first Jockey Club, which became known as the Kentucky Jockey Club in 1809.

Question 6: What three-year-old chestnut colt was the first Kentucky Derby winner?
a) Hindoo
b) Aristides
c) Day Star
d) Vagrant

Question 7: Name the first horse to win the Triple Crown races: the Kentucky Derby, Preakness, and Belmont Stakes.
a) Man o' War
b) Lexington
c) Regret
d) Sir Barton

Question 8: In 1925, *New York Times* and *New York Journal-American* sports columnist, Bill Corum, who later became president of Churchill Downs from 1950-58, first used the famous phrase, "Run for the _____."
a) Lillies
b) Daisies
c) Hills

d) Roses

Question 9: Name the 1973 Kentucky Derby winner who went on to become the first Triple Crown winner in 25 years.
   a) Secretariat
   b) Seattle Slew
   c) Affirmed
   d) Genuine Risk

Question 10: What song is traditionally played by the University of Louisville Marching Band just moments before the start of the Kentucky Derby?

ANSWER KEY

6. B. Aristides was the first Kentucky Derby winner.

7. D. In 1919, Sir Barton became the first horse to win the Triple Crown.

8. D. Roses.

9. A. Secretariat.

10. B. Pat Day.

Question 11: Name the Kentucky Derby winning horse that was purchased for $4 million by Fusao Sekiguchi at the Keeneland Yearling Sales.
   a) Big Brown
   b) Fusaichi Pegasus
   c) Barbaro
   d) Giacomo

Question 12: This jockey, who grew up in Colorado dreaming of becoming a cowboy, went on to be Kentucky's all-time leading rider at Churchill Downs and Keeneland. He once rode eight winners in one afternoon at Arlington Park in Illinois.
   a) Kent Desormeaux
   b) Pat Day
   c) Mike E. Smith
   d) Bill Shoemaker

Question 13: Name the legendary basketball coach who is the lead partner in Celtic Pride Stable and the Ol Memorial Stable. HINT: He is best known for coaching the NBA's New York Knicks and Boston Celtics and the 1996 NCAA champion University of Kentucky Wildcats. Currently, he coaches for the University of Louisville. He is the first coach to take three different teams to the Final Four (Providence, Kentucky and Louisville).

Question 14: In 2011, jockey John R. Velazquez rode this Team Valor horse to victory in the 137th Kentucky Derby in front of a then record crowd of 164,858. Velazquez was originally scheduled to ride Uncle Mo, but the favorite and American Champion Two-Year-Old Male Horse was scratched due to an illness.
  a) Animal Kingdom
  b) Santiva
  c) Shackleford
  d) Twinspired
  e) Zenyatta

Question 15: How old are all the horses that run in the Kentucky Derby?

ANSWER KEY

11. B. Fusaichi Pegasus was purchased for $4 million.

12. The Stephen Foster ballad "My Old Kentucky Home."

13. Rick Pitino. Pitino's best horses were Hallory Hunter (fourth place at 1998 Kentucky Derby) and AP Valentine (winner of Champagne Stakes 2000).

14. A. Animal Kingdom. The first time Velazquez rode Animal Kingdom was in the Kentucky Derby and it was Velazquez's first Derby win in 13 tries.

15. All the horses that run in the Kentucky Derby are three-year-olds.

2 LAYING THE TRACKS FOR CHURCHILL DOWNS

"The crowd in the grandstand sent out a volume of voice, and the crowd in the field took it up and carried it from boundary to boundary of Churchill Downs."
— *Louisville Commercial*, 1883

PERHAPS IT ALL STARTED in 1779 when the 12th Earl of Derby and Sir Charles Bunbury saw the first running of the Epsom Oaks in England. Inspired, the two were determined to start their own race the following year. They flipped a coin for naming rights and Lord Derby won.

Years later, when Kentuckians created their own version of the race using the Epsom Derby as the model, The Kentucky Derby was born and one of the richest histories in sports began.

You are likely to get a slow start out of the gate and may get blocked by the 20-horse, talented Kentucky Derby field. This is likely the toughest chapter in the book, so do not be discouraged.

Get to the rail and stay the course.

Question 16: True or False: The first horse racetrack in Kentucky was in 1775 at Churchill Downs.

Question 17: To avoid problems associated with racing in Louisville's busy downtown area on Market Street, a racetrack was created on Shippingport Island in 1805. Name the track that was on this island in the Ohio River.
a) Oakland Race Course
b) Hope Distillery Course
c) Elm Tree Gardens
d) Beargrass Track
e) Yum-Yum

Question 18: This course was developed in 1827 on what is currently Main and 16th Streets.
a) Oakland Race Course
b) Hope Distillery Course
c) Elm Tree Gardens
d) Beargrass Track
e) Lynn's Paradise Course

Question 19: Oftentimes races were held on private farms in the early 1800s. One of the more famous of these was Peter Funk's:
a) Oakland Race Course
b) Hope Distillery Course
c) Elm Tree Gardens
d) P.W. Reese Racetrack
e) Beargrass Track

Question 20: "Old Louisville" boasts the site of this track that was opened in the fall of 1833. It was located in the area now known as Seventh and Magnolia Streets.
a) Oakland Racetrack
b) Hope Distillery Course
c) Elm Tree Gardens
d) Hunter S. Thompson Track
e) Beargrass Track

ANSWER KEY

16. False. Horse racing in Kentucky dates back to 1789. The first racetrack was created in Lexington.

17. C. Elm Tree Gardens.

18. B. Hope Distillery Course.

19. E. Beargrass Track.

20. A. Oakland Racetrack.

Question 21: In 1858, Woodlawn Course opened on the Louisville and Lexington railroad near the area known today as East Louisville's St. Matthews. Although the track closed in 1870, the track's trophy known as the Woodlawn Vase is presented to the winner of what prestigious race?

Question 22: In 1868, what harness racing track was built just east of Churchill Downs?
a) Greeneland
b) Keeneland
c) Hope Distillery Course
d) Zachary Taylor Track
e) Beargrass Track

Question 23: What is Colonel M. Lewis Clark, Jr.'s first name?

Question 24: Clark was the grandson of what famous explorer and Missouri governor?

Question 25: Colonel M. Lewis Clark traveled in England and France in 1872 and 1873. He met England's Admiral Rous and France's Vicompte Darn and other racing visionaries. How old was Clark when he first dreamed the idea of a Louisville Jockey Club that would ultimately lead to the development of Churchill Downs?
  a) 26
  b) 33
  c) 46
  d) 57

ANSWER KEY

21. Since 1917, the winner of the Preakness Stakes at Pimlico has been presented the Woodlawn Vase trophy.

22. A. Greeneland.

23. Meriwether.

24. Colonel M. Lewis Clark, Jr. was the grandson of General William Clark of the Lewis and Clark Expedition. His father was Major Meriwether Lewis Clark, Sr. His mother was Abigail Prather Churchill.

25. A. 26.

Question 26: Where did Clark and other Louisville gentlemen meet on June 18, 1874, to discuss the development of the Louisville Jockey Club?

Question 27: How many acres of land did M. Lewis Clark lease from his uncles John and Henry Churchill to construct a clubhouse, grandstand, porter's lodge, and six stables that eventually led to the opening of the tracks?
  a) 40
  b) 80
  c) 110
  d) 200

Question 28: Clark financed the initial construction of the track by selling membership subscriptions to the track at $100 each. How many memberships did he sell?

Question 29: Because the track faced financial woes, the New Louisville Jockey Club was incorporated in 1894. M. Lewis Clark remained as the track's presiding judge. Club President William F. Schulte constructed a $100,000 grandstand on the opposite side of the track. What is significant about this grandstand's architectural elements?

Question 30: Clark modeled his three major stakes races after England's three prestigious races the Epsom Derby, Epsom Oaks, and St. Leger Stakes. What did Clark call his races?

ANSWER KEY

26. The Galt House. In 2009, the Galt House Hotel, located on the waterfront of the Ohio River, signed a three-year sponsorship agreement with Churchill Downs to be named the "Official Host Hotel of Churchill Downs, the Kentucky Derby, and the Kentucky Oaks."

27. B. 80.

28. Clark sold 320 memberships at $100 each to finance the $32,000 track construction project.

29. The grandstand's twin spires constructed on the roof would become the symbol of Churchill Downs and the Kentucky Derby.

30. The Kentucky Derby, Kentucky Oaks, and Clark Handicap.

Question 31: True or False: Clark's three major races have been conducted in the spring since 1875.

Question 32: Facing financial issues in 1902, a group consisting of Charles Price, tailor Matt J. Winn, and what Louisville politician began operating the track?

Question 33: The first reference of "Churchill Downs" was reported in the *Louisville Commercial* in the ninth Derby in 1883: "The crowd in the grandstand sent out a volume of voice, and the crowd in the field took it up and carried it from boundary to boundary of Churchill Downs." However, the track was not incorporated as Churchill Downs until what year?
   a) 1885

b) 1911
c) 1919
d) 1937

Question 34: In 1918 and 1919, a group led by James Graham Brown took over Churchill Downs and what other three racetracks in Kentucky?
a) Douglas Park, Latonia, and the Kentucky Association
b) Keeneland, Greeneland, and Oakland Racetrack
c) Lincoln Fields, Arlington, Red Mile
d) Keeneland, Fairmount, and Douglas Park

Question 35: What is the name of the association that took over Churchill Downs on January 16, 1928?

ANSWER KEY

31. False. In 1953, the Clark Handicap began running in the fall.

32. In 1902, Mayor Charles Grainger was named president.

33. D. 1937.

34. Douglas Park, Latonia, and the Kentucky Association.

35. American Turf Association took over Churchill Downs in 1928.

Question 36: This association also served as the holding company for all of the following Kentucky and Illinois tracks except for which one?
a) Douglas Park
b) Latonia
c) Lincoln Fields
d) Arlington
e) Washington Park

Question 37: In 1948, President Matt Winn, other board members and a committee explored operating the track as a non-profit organization to donate its earnings to what institution?

Question 38: Churchill Downs Foundation, a charitable organization led by J. Graham Brown, conducted several races each fall for charitable purposes resulting in in the donation of how much money during a ten-year period in the 1940-50s?
a) $250,000

b) $500,000
c) $1,500,000
d) $2,000,000

Question 39: What Churchill Downs president took over for the retiring Wathen Knebelkamp in 1969 and lead the track in the 1970s and 1980s?

Question 40: Who is William Whitley and why is he such a significant figure for Kentucky horseracing?

ANSWER KEY

36. D. Arlington.

37. University of Louisville School of Medicine.

38. C. $1,500,000.

39. Lynn Stone.

40. William Whitley was an American pioneer and an important figure in the early settlement of Kentucky. He fought in both the Indian wars and War of 1812, but his most significant legacy with Kentucky horseracing is that he laid out a racetrack in 1788 near present day Harrodsburg, Kentucky. Because Whitley vehemently opposed the British and disapproved of their customs, he insisted that his racetrack be opposite of theirs. The British preferred turf tracks, so he built his racetrack with clay, thus creating the first racetrack in America to consist of clay. Instead of running his races clockwise like they run in England, he ran his races counter-clockwise.

3 THE NUMBERS

"With your throat dry from cheering ... you look down at the winning ticket in your hand, and no matter how large the payoff or whether you won by a whim or careful calculation, the greatest thing is to know you're still lucky."
— Sheri Seggerman and Mary Tiegreen, *The Kentucky Derby: 101 Reasons to Love America's Favorite Horse Race*

WERE YOU SLOW OUT of the Chapter 2 gates? Don't fret. 2011 Derby champion Animal Kingdom went from last to first and you can too. At the very least, you can muster a respectable race the rest of the way and at least finish in the money!

Question 41: How many people watched the first Kentucky Derby on May 17, 1875?
  a) 10,000
  b) 15,000
  c) 30,000
  d) 45,000

Question 42: W. F. Schulte purchased the track in 1894 and built another grandstand. How high was this grandstand?
  a) 150 feet
  b) 215 feet
  c) 250 feet
  d) 285 feet

Question 43: In 1896, the Kentucky Derby was shortened from 1 ½ miles to 1 ¼ miles. Why was the distance adjusted?

Question 44: Of the first 28 Kentucky Derbys, how many were won by African-American jockeys?
  a) 5
  b) 10
  c) 15
  d) 26

Question 45: In 1914, Old Rosebud set a track record of 2:03 2/5 and won the Derby by how many lengths?
  a) 5

b) 6
c) 7
d) 8

ANSWER KEY

41. A. An estimated 10,000 spectators viewed the first running of the Kentucky Derby.

42. B. 285 feet.

43. The Kentucky Derby was shortened to 1 ¼ miles because 1 ½ miles was considered too long for three-year-olds to race so early in the cooler spring weather.

44. C. 15.

45. D. 8.

Question 46: In 1943, World War II travel restrictions prohibited Churchill Downs from selling tickets to out-of-towners. How many spectators witnessed Count Fleet, a favorite, pick up an easy win in what was called the "Street Car Derby"?
   a) 50,000
   b) 65,000
   c) 70,000
   d) 75,000

Question 47: What were the odds for 1943 Kentucky Derby winner Count Fleet?
   a) 2-5
   b) 4-5
   c) 1-1
   d) 2-1

Question 48: Count Fleet went on to win the Preakness by eight lengths. By how many lengths did he win the Belmont?
   a) 8
   b) 12
   c) 18
   d) 25

Question 49: How many stakes races did Citation win in 1948, the year he won the Triple Crown?

    a) 8

    b) 12

    c) 14

    d) 17

Question 50: Col. Matt J. Winn, President of Churchill Downs from 1938-49, died October 6, 1949, at the age of 88. How many Kentucky Derby races did he witness?

    a) 50

    b) 60

    c) 70

    d) 75

ANSWER KEY

46. B. 65,000.

47. A. Count Fleet was 2-5 favorite and won by three lengths.

48. D. 25! Count Fleet's 25-length victory at the Belmont was a record that stood until 1973.

49. D. Citation won an astounding 17 stakes races!

50. D. 75. Winn witnessed each of the first 75 Derbys. At age 13, he watched his first Derby in the infield from his father's grocery wagon.

ABOUT THE AUTHOR

JOEL KATTE is the author of the Amazon #1 Best-Selling *Milwaukee Brewers IQ: The Ultimate Test of True Fandom*. Joel's other books include:

Green Bay Packers IQ: The Ultimate Test of True Fandom
Kentucky Derby IQ: The Ultimate Test of True Fandom
St. Louis Cardinals IQ: The Ultimate Test of True Fandom (Volume 1, with Larry Underwood)

Joel's most recent book in Black Mesa's best-selling trivia and history series is *University of Kentucky Wildcats Basketball IQ: The Ultimate Test of True Fandom*. It was released in March 2016.

After playing one year of minor league baseball in the California Angels system, Joel graduated from Lakeland College and became a high school English teacher. He then earned his Masters degree from Aurora University and worked as an elementary school principal for nine years. Currently, Joel works as a district administrator for four alternative school special programs in Lexington, Kentucky.

Joel is writing about his experiences as a player and fan in his memoir *The County Stadium Kid*. He also continues to work on other IQ titles for Black Mesa and will be releasing *Summer Olympics IQ: The Ultimate Test of True Fandom* in spring 2016.

To inquire about author visits for schools, organizations or teams, please call (859) 967-9508 or email JoelKatte@gmail.com. For updates follow Joel on Twitter: @joelkatte

BLACK MESA

Black Mesa is a Florida-based publishing company that specializes in sports trivia and history. To purchase in bulk or to use this or any of our other titles as a fundraiser for your organization, club or team, please contact:

admin@blackmesabooks.com

Visit us on the Web for updated book information and to meet our authors:

www.blackmesabooks.com

REFERENCES

Books

The Cats' Pause: 2015-16 Kentucky Basketball Yearbook. Lexington, KY: 2015.

Clark, Ryan, and Joe Cox. *100 Things Wildcats Fans Should Know and Do Before They Die.* Chicago: Triumph Books LLC, 2012.

Wallace, Tom. *University of Kentucky Basketball Encyclopedia.* Champaign, IL: Sports Publishing, 2012.

Newspapers

The Lexington Herald-Leader

The Courier-Journal

Websites

Basketball-Reference.com

BigBlueHistory.net

BleacherReport.com

CoachCal.com

Espn.go.com

NBA.com

Sports-Reference.com

Tjcaa.org

Twitter.com

UKAthletics.com

admin@blackmesabooks.com
www.blackmesabooks.com

CPSIA information can be obtained
at www.ICGtesting.com
Printed in the USA
LVOW13s2147180617
538562LV00009B/554/P